The MVS Primer

Computer Books from QED

Systems Development
The Complete Guide to Software Testing
Developing Client/Server Applications
Quality Assurance for Information Systems
User-Interface Screen Design
On Time, Within Budget: Software Project Management Practices and Techniques
Managing Software Projects: Selecting and Using PC-Based Project Management Systems
From Mainframe to Workstations: Offloading Application Development
A Structured Approach to Systems Testing
Rapid Application Prototyping: The Storyboard Approach to User Requirements Analysis
Software Engineering with Formal Metrics
Testing Client/Server Applications
Making Software Measurement Work: Building an Effective Measurement Program

Information Engineering/CASE
Practical Model Management Using CASE Tools
Building the Data Warehouse
Information Systems Architecture: Development in the 90's
Enterprise Architecture Planning: Developing a Blueprint for Data, Applications, and Technology
Data Architecture: The Information Paradigm

IBM Systems Software
REXX in the TSO Environment
REXX Tools and Techniques
The MVS Primer
Cross System Product Application Development
TSO/E CLISTS: The Complete Tutorial and Reference Guide
MVS/JCL: Mastering Job Control Language
MVS/VSAM for the Application Programmer
Introduction to Cross System Product
CICS: A How-To for COBOL Programmers
CICS: A Guide to Performance Tuning
CICS Application and System Programming: Tools and Techniques
CICS: A Guide to Application Debugging

OS/2
Thinking Person's Guide to Using OS/2 2.1
OS/2 Presentation Manager Programming for COBOL Programmers
OS/2 C Programming

Programming – Micro Focus
Micro Focus COBOL Workbench for the Application Developer
Micro Focus CICS Option 3.0

Programming – C
Learn C and Save Your Job: C Language for COBOL Programmers
C Pointers and Dynamic Memory Management
Developing Portable System Call Libraries Using C

AS/400
AS/400: A Practical Guide for Programming and Operations
AS/400 Architecture and Applications: The Database Machine

UNIX
UNIX C Shell Desk Reference
The UNIX Industry and Open Systems in Transition

Management and Operations
Total Quality Management in Information Services
The Disaster Recovery Plan
Controlling the Future: Managing Technology-Driven Change
How to Automate Your Computer Center
Mind Your Business: Managing the Impact of End-User Computing
Understanding Data Pattern Processing: The Key to Competitive Advantage
The Software Factory: Managing Software Development and Maintenance
Ethical Conflicts in Information and Computer Sciences, Technology, and Business
Strategic and Operational Planning for Information Services
Object Technology and Distributed Computing

VAX/VMS
Rdb/VMS: Developing the Data Warehouse
Network Programming Under DECNet Phases IV and V
VAX/VMS: Mastering DCL Commands and Utilities

Database
Client/Server and Distributed Database Design
Third-Wave Processing: Database Machines and Decision Support Systems
Database Management Systems: Understanding and Applying Database Technology

Database — DB2
QMF: How to Use Query Management Facility with DB2 and SQL/DS
SQL for DB2 and SQL/DS Application Developers
DB2: the Complete Guide to Implementation and Use
Embedded SQL for DB2: Application Design and Development
DB2: Maximizing Performance in Online Production Systems

QED books are available at special quantity discounts for educational uses, premiums, and sales promotions. Special books, book excerpts, and instructive materials can be created to meet specific needs.

This is Only a Partial Listing. For Additional Information or a Free Catalog contact
QED Publishing Group • P. O. Box 812070 • Wellesley, MA 02181-0013
Telephone: 617-237-5656 or fax 617-235-0826

The MVS Primer

David Shelby Kirk

QED Technical Publishing Group
Boston • Toronto • London

© 1992 QED Information Sciences, Inc.
P.O. Box 82-181
Wellesley, MA 02181

QED Technical Publishing Group is a division of QED Information Sciences, Inc.

All rights reserved. No part of the material protected by this copyright notice may be reproduced or utilized in any form or by any means, electronic or mechanical, including photocopying, recording, or by any information storage and retrieval system without written permission from the copyright owner.

Library of Congress Catalog Number: 91-34014
International Standard Book Number: 0-89435-3993

Printed in the United States of America
    93 94 10 9 8 7 6 5 4 3 2

Library of Congress Cataloging-in-Publication Data

Kirk, David Shelby.
    The MVS primer / David Shelby Kirk.
      p.   cm.
    Includes index.
    ISBN 0-89435-399-3
    1. Systems software. 2. MVS (Computer system) I. Title.
QA76.76.S95K57 1992
005.4'429—dc20

Dedication

This book is dedicated to beginning programmers everywhere who hoped to be professional programmers once they knew a programming language. I hope this book helps them unravel many of the complexities they will face as they work in a large corporate MVS computing environment.

I also dedicate this book to all the systems programmers with whom I shared many long days and longer nights during my career; they are the people who gave to MVS its quality reputation. I've never known a systems programmer who worked only a 40-hour week, and I doubt that I ever will. The job is too demanding for anything less than a full commitment to the task. My years spent in systems programming were some of my happiest, where I learned the value of initiative and of teamwork.

Contents

List of Figures xi
Preface xiii
Acknowledgments to IBM Products xvii

CHAPTER 1. FUNCTIONS OF MVS 1
  1.1. JOB MANAGEMENT 3
      1.1.1. JES 4
      1.1.2. JCL 5
      1.1.3. System flowcharts 8
  1.2. TASK MANAGEMENT 10
  1.3. DATA MANAGEMENT 15
      1.3.1. Access methods 15
      1.3.2. Handling the I/O 17
      1.3.3. Using the catalog 21
  1.4. ENVIRONMENT CONTROL 24
      1.4.1. Telecommunications and transaction systems 24
      1.4.2. Time-sharing services 28
      1.4.3. Security 29
      1.4.4. Accounting and monitoring 30

CHAPTER 2. HISTORY OF OPERATING SYSTEMS 35
  2.1. PREOPERATING SYSTEM WORLD 35
  2.2. SECOND-GENERATION MACHINES 38
      2.2.1. Programming languages 39

viii   THE MVS PRIMER

    2.2.2.   Program libraries 42
    2.2.3.   Use of JCL to isolate jobs..42
    2.2.4.   Need for multiprogramming as a cost control agent 43

CHAPTER 3. HISTORY OF MVS 47
  3.1.   S/360 ANNOUNCEMENT 48
    3.1.1.   Hardware interrupts and their purpose 49
    3.1.2.   Fixed addresses for program services (SVCs) 51
    3.1.3.   I/O data channels 52
    3.1.4.   Instruction set and registers 53
  3.2.   OS COMPONENTS 55
    3.2.1.   OS/360 — the basics 56
    3.2.2.   System administration — utilities 58
    3.2.3.   Programming facilities and libraries 59
  3.3.   OS TO MVS EVOLUTION 63
    3.3.1.   Memory management 65
    3.3.2.   Emergence of MVS job scheduling facilities 68
    3.3.3.   Emergence of online and database facilities 71

CHAPTER 4. ONLINE ACCESS AND DATABASES 75
  4.1.   TSO 75
  4.2.   IMS and DL/I 76
  4.3.   CICS 82
  4.4.   DB2 and SQL 84

CHAPTER 5. MVS TODAY 91
  5.1.   MVS VARIATIONS 91
  5.2.   MVS COMPONENTS 94
    5.2.1.   Data repository 95
    5.2.2.   Distributed data 95
    5.2.3.   IMS, DB2, and CICS integration 96
    5.2.4.   The role of assembler language 97
    5.2.5.   Packaging of access methods 99

CHAPTER 6. LEARNING MVS 103
  6.1.   MVS PROGRAMMER SKILL REQUIREMENTS 105
  6.2.   MVS ANALYST SKILL REQUIREMENTS 107
  6.3.   MVS MIS MANAGER SKILL REQUIREMENTS 108
  6.4   MVS END USER SKILL REQUIREMENTS 110
  6.5.   SUGGESTED READING APPROACH 110

APPENDIX. MISCELLANEOUS REFERENCE SECTION 113
GLOSSARY OF TERMS 113
SKILL MATRIX FOR TYPICAL CAREER POSITIONS 115
PUBLICATIONS AVAILABLE 116
From QED 116
From IBM 118

Index 123

List of Figures

Figure		Page
1.1.	JES job flow.	5
1.2.	Example of JCL.	6
1.3.	Sample system flowchart.	9
1.4.	Example of multiple tasks sharing CPU.	13
1.5.	Example of overloaded CPU.	14
1.6.	Sample computer configuration.	18
1.7.	Sample catalog and VTOC structure.	22
1.8.	Conceptual telecommunications view.	26
2.1.	Overview of computer generations.	39
2.2.	Example of machine language versus Autocoder language.	40
2.3	Example of second-generation job control.	43
3.1.	Concept of hardware interrupt process.	50
3.2.	Second- versus third-generation instructions.	55
3.3.	Example of the two-step compile/link process	60
3.4.	Example of PDS concepts.	61
3.5.	Evolution of OS to MVS.	63
3.6.	Comparison of SVS and MVS.	65
3.7.	Example of virtual storage.	67

xi

Figure		*Page*
3.8.	Example of JES2 job flow.	69
3.9.	Example of JES3 facilities.	70
4.1.	Example of IMS database structure.	77
4.2.	Example of IMS database record.	78
4.3.	Example of online transaction screen.	79
4.4.	Example of CICS and COBOL compile steps.	83
4.5.	Example of relational data structure.	86
5.1.	Example of multiple ESA address spaces.	93
5.2.	Example of a Sysplex structure.	94
5.3.	Example of APPC with SNA network.	96
5.4.	Example of shared IMS, CICS, and DB2 system.	97
5.5.	Example of assembler program.	98

Preface

WHAT THIS BOOK IS:

This book presents a conceptual view of what is probably the largest and best-known proprietary operating system in use today, IBM's MVS software family. I wrote this book for the reader who understands (and probably uses) computers but does not know what operating systems do, why they exist, or how the component parts are structured. This book addresses those issues within the context of MVS and is meant for managers, programmers, and end users who work with MVS applications. Persons who do not work with MVS will find the book of some value for its conceptual presentation, since most operating systems in use today (including those for PCs) have some resemblance to what appears here.

Although the title of this book references MVS, there is also information on the many other components that typically constitute an MVS installation. While the information on these other components is not very detailed, the inclusion was necessary to present a useful picture of the MVS *family*. IMS, TSO, DB2, and CICS are what most readers face in their day-to-day contact with MVS. Understanding how these products relate to MVS is an important building block to grasping the complexity of the MVS world. Programmers and computer operators are seldom among the professionals to directly interact with the operating system and with the hardware itself. For that reason, and also for the possible curiosity of other readers, I included some of the conceptual aspects of the hardware and how it makes it possible for there to be an MVS at all.

WHAT THIS BOOK IS NOT:

This is an introductory text, not a technical reference. This book does not contain the details needed to develop system specifications or to write applications. It makes no claim to thoroughness or even technical accuracy in discussing certain topics. This license was necessary to condense volumes of material into an easy-to-understand format. Chapter 7 contains lists of other reading material, both from QED and IBM, that will supply more information.

HOW THIS BOOK IS ORGANIZED:

Chapter 1. Functions of MVS. This first chapter explains what MVS does. This is to ensure that you, the reader, understand what services are performed by MVS. Applying this information to your job is not dependent on what is presented in later chapters. This chapter does not, however, explain how MVS works and what the various components are, topics you should know before you can use this information for maximum effectiveness. They are discussed in later chapters.

Chapter 2. History of Operating Systems. This chapter is designed to help you understand how the functions performed by MVS evolved through need and how necessary the functions are today to achieve a cost-effective operation. Although this chapter could be considered optional, it helps build a foundation for understanding operating systems.

Chapter 3. History of MVS. This chapter covers the growth of MVS since its announcement by IBM in 1964 (known then as OS). As new components are added, you will watch MVS grow from a batch-oriented environment of basic job management to a high volume online transaction manager for mission-critical corporate systems.

Chapter 4. Online Access and Databases. This chapter provides more information on some major components normally found in MVS environments, including IMS, TSO, CICS, and DB2. This chapter presents some of their features and functions.

Chapter 5. MVS Today. This is the world of MVS with which you are probably most familiar. This chapter will review the various MVS components in use today and how they typically interact in an installation. This chapter builds on information that was introduced in Chapters 3 and 4.

Chapter 6. Learning MVS. Since MVS is so enormous and so complex, many people avoid any effort to learn about it. This chapter offers some guidelines on how to approach the task of learning more about MVS by tailoring suggestions to typical job titles. This chapter can also assist anyone who must develop training curriculums for MIS personnel.

Appendix. Reference Section. This final chapter contains information that may be of use as you become more skilled in interacting in an MVS environment. There is a glossary and some skill matrices that will assist you in using the system.

WHO THIS BOOK IS FOR:

When I first began work on this book, I assumed the reader would be a novice programmer or student. As the book took shape, I realized that there are many other people who could appreciate such a book: the MIS managers who learned programming in a simpler age; the end users who work with online systems; the analysts who attempt to cope with the issues of IMS, CICS, and other application environment opportunities; and even experienced programmers who work in an MVS shop but don't understand what happens to the programs they write. All of these people need a text that will help them tie the many components together

Can you afford to work with MVS without reading this book? Yes, you can. But not if you're frustrated by terms such as JCL, JES, VSAM, IMS, and would like to know how they fit into the overall scheme of a data center. This book won't give you basic survival skills. You already have those. In fact, that's why you chose this book in the first place. This book will make you more self-reliant in your use of the system, in deciding what components should be part of new applications, and in determining what new skills would benefit you the most.

The book includes some vignettes about people who work in MVS systems. I did this to remind you, the reader, that an MVS data center is flesh and blood, not just bits and bytes. Working with MVS can affect the professional and personal lives of those who are closest to it. MVS is a success not only because of its software and technology but also because of the many dedicated people who work with it.

In each chapter, in each paragraph, I have attempted to present useful information. If I've omitted some pertinent topic, made an error, or included information that you haven't found to be useful, please let me know. There is a response form in the back of the book, and I would enjoy hearing from you.

David Shelby Kirk
Cicero, New York

Acknowledgments To IBM Products

Because this book focuses on the IBM hardware and software environment, I have tried to present the major aspects of various components while avoiding technical material that might distract readers. Since the book makes generic references to various components, I feel obligated to share with you the proper names of the products I worked with in developing this book.

Term used in book	*IBM product*
MVS	Multiple Virtual Storage — MVS/SP, MVS/XA, and MVS/ESA unless noted
CICS	Customer Information Control System (CICS/OS/VS, CICS/MVS, and CICS/ESA)
IMS	Information Management System (IMS/VS and IMS/ESA)
DB2	DATABASE 2
ISPF	Interactive Structured Programming Facility

The following terms used in this book are trademarks of International Business Machines Corporation:

MVS/SP, MVS/XA, MVS/ESA, IBM, SAA, OS/2, OS/400, CICS/MVS, DB2, DATABASE 2, QMF, VTAM, PS/2,

AS/400, Systems Application Architecture, CICS/ESA, IMS/ESA, System/360, System/370, Repository Manager/MVS

The time: Sunday night, 8:00 P.M.

The location: A typical MVS data center

The systems programmers had just returned from getting a quick pizza and a couple of beers. The fresh air had raised their spirits, but the pizza had been a little too spicy. The night's work was still ahead of them, and they had already put in a long day. So far, they had applied all of the PTFs and APARs that were on the weekend plan, but they still needed to re-IPL with the new library and JCL changes. When the operators and shift supervisor saw the jeans-clad crew shuffling into the computer room, they put down their stained coffee mugs and flipped a coin for the last stale doughnut. It was time to bring up MVS and start the night's processing cycle. Monday morning would soon be here.

Things hadn't gone well all week. IMS had crashed three times when a new application had been hurried into production, and response time for CICS had been the pits for days. No one seemed to have the solution for that. DASD space was nonexistent and those darn application programmers ate it up like it was candy. IBM had just shipped the latest upgrade to COBOL, and one of the project managers had been screaming for days that her project was late because she didn't have a couple of the new features. It had been a typical week.

The mainframe had been powered down for a couple of hours while IBM engineers upgraded some components and did some preventive maintenance. The systems programmers hadn't missed this chance to bug out for the pizza. That had been an unexpected treat. The engineers were packing their tools away now, and the mainframe was sitting quietly. Without software, it was just so much electronic circuitry with less intelligence than a digital watch.

After reviewing status with the engineers (some scheduled upgrades to a DASD controller hadn't been applied due to time constraints, and the intermittent parity error was still unresolved), the systems programmers and shift supervisor agreed that it wasn't going to get any better so they might as well fire it up. They reviewed the list of temporary adjustments to make at IPL, and one of the operators pressed the LOAD key.

On that instruction, the mainframe executed what little intelligence it had, not unlike the dog that shakes your hand but knows no other tricks. Using preprogrammed code in ROM, the mainframe executed a read operation to the designated DASD and read the IPL record into memory. At that point, the systems programmers knew one thing would happen: MVS would either fly or die. With so many changes — most tested but some not — you could never be sure of the outcome. Whereas application software worked under the protective umbrella of MVS, MVS had to build the umbrella. If MVS didn't start up, the systems programmers would work through the night to restore a backup IPL volume and try again. It wouldn't be the first time. It was either that or the company employees may as well stay home on Monday morning — and there would be hell to pay if that happened.

Suddenly, status messages began to appear on the operator's terminal screen as MVS slowly came to life. Once again, MVS was beginning the process of rediscovering itself and checking out the mainframe configuration. In another 15 to 20 minutes, it would be ready for another week's work. Maybe tonight wouldn't be so bad. The operators went to get the job sheets for the night's schedule. The systems programmers started setting up some tests to trap that IMS bug. Another week in the world of MVS had begun.

1

Functions of MVS

When you decided to read this book, you were probably wondering, "What is MVS?" There is no simple answer to that question; it will evolve in the course of the book. This first chapter discusses what MVS does, establishing a good foundation for absorbing and using later topics dealt with in the book. As you progress through the chapters, you may want to occasionally revisit this chapter to review some of MVS's functions.

The previous paragraph didn't answer your immediate question, did it? You still want to know what MVS stands for. Okay, here goes. MVS stands for *Multiple Virtual Storage*. Not much use, is it? That's my point. Knowing the real name of MVS doesn't help you understand why it has that name, what it does, or how to use it to advantage. This book will address all those issues, but questions about MVS have no simple answers.

Before proceeding, let's review some basic terminology that is used frequently with mainframe computers. Assuming that you already know computer fundamentals, whether these terms are used at your company isn't as important as being familiar with the concepts.

Batch versus *online* A batch process is one that is scheduled by people, whereas an online process is one that occurs whenever a person operates a

1

2 THE MVS PRIMER

terminal that is attached to the computer. Batch processes will normally represent a large unit of work, such as preparing a company's payroll. An online process is usually a specific request by a single person. This might be an inquiry typed into a terminal to verify an employee number or to change a customer's mailing address. To MVS, the major difference is that batch work is scheduled, whereas online work is done on demand.

CPU The component of the computer that does logic processing. This is separate from memory (where programs and data may be stored while a program is using the CPU) or peripheral data devices (where programs and data may be stored for long periods).

Dataset, file, or *database* These terms refer to a collection of related data that is entered into a storage device such as disk or tape. This might be a file of customer names, a file of salary ranges by job title, or a large database of a parts inventory and suppliers. We will use the term that is most appropriate, although a database usually refers to a collection of integrated files or to a file that also contains structural information that is beyond the scope of this book.

Other terms used throughout the book are those commonly used in the computing profession and include such terms as byte, bit, data center, programmer, operator, tape reel, disk storage, I/O, and binary. No detailed explanation of these terms is offered in the book. If any of these terms are unfamiliar to you, I suggest you first read an introductory text on computers and then return to this book.

If your only exposure to computers is desktop computers (PCs), some of the material covered in this book may appear foreign. You may find that the book makes more sense if you skip immediately to Chapter 2 and then resume here afterwards. I make this suggestion because PCs, because they serve one user, share many of the processes and problems of early mainframe computers. (Note: That is changing. PCs of the future will share many of the features of MVS. Already, some have various degrees of job, task, and data management facilities.)

The next sections will present the major components of MVS, highlighting the features of managing jobs, tasks, and data within the computer center. You will see how MVS manages the entire computing environment, ranging from the scheduling of batch processes to coordinating the sharing of system resources for online access. Learning MVS takes time and patience. Enjoy the trip.

1.1. JOB MANAGEMENT

Job management is the most elementary in concept and usually the most visible of the many functions performed by MVS. Although simple in concept, job management may well be the most complex technically. A job is elementary in concept only because it represents how people define and view the work processed by MVS.

First, let's define the term *job*. A job is a collection of pro cesses that accomplish a business function. Ouch! That didn't help, did it? Let's try again: A job is a set of work that the computer is to do for a given user or department. Better? Not much. Let's not beat the dictionary to death. Instead, here are some examples that demonstrate the concept of a job.

Prepare a payroll:

Processes: 1. Sort employee data alphabetically by department.

2. Calculate gross pay and deductions for each employee.

3. Print a payroll register for each department.

4. Print paychecks for each employee.

Update employee files:

Processes: 1. Validate information for new employees (e.g., sex code should be M or F, department code should be a valid code for the company).

2. Add data for employees to company employee database.

3. Print name lists for each department.

Each of the above examples represents a business function for a business unit, in this case the payroll department. Each of the numbered processes might be a separate computer program and processed in sequence. A sequential process within a job is known as a *step*. A job, then, consists of one or more steps.

The major issue to understand is that the two jobs are independent of each other. MVS schedules the two jobs such that the steps for each are viewed as separate units within their respective jobs. This lets users of an MVS system plan only for their own work and not other work that MVS may be handling. For example, every other Friday the payroll department might request that the data center process the job that prepares the payroll. The other job, however, might be processed every day if there are frequently new employees, promotions, or pay and job changes.

1.1.1. JES

When jobs enter the MVS system, they are processed by the Job Entry Subsystem (JES, pronounced *jez*). JES is an MVS component and usually one of the first that users encounter. JES validates jobs and prepares them for scheduling by task management (next topic). When the job terminates, JES is there to coordinate distribution and printing of any reports that may have been produced. See Figure 1.1.

(Note: Were you surprised when I gave you the pronunciation for the acronym? Don't be. Experienced MVS users pronounce all acronyms, even those with no vowels. You'll know you've "got it" when you start pronouncing the acronyms as though they were words.)

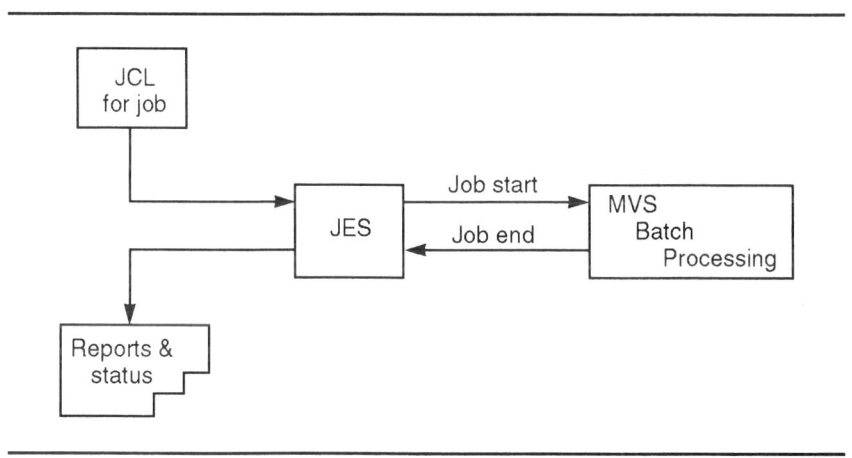

```
   ┌─────────┐
   │  JCL    │
   │ for job │
   └────┬────┘
        │
        ▼           Job start    ┌──────────────┐
      ┌─────┐ ──────────────────▶│    MVS       │
      │ JES │                    │   Batch      │
      └──┬──┘ ◀──────────────────│  Processing  │
         │        Job end        └──────────────┘
         ▼
   ┌──────────┐
   │ Reports &│
   │  status  │
   └──────────┘
```

Figure 1.1. JES job flow.

1.1.2. JCL

MVS doesn't know job processing requirements by itself. People give MVS instructions. Such instructions are prepared in a specialized computer language known as Job Control Language (JCL). Virtually every unit of work done by an MVS-controlled computer is identified by JCL. For example, while you usually don't need to be aware of JES, there are some special JCL commands that some installations use to take advantage of special JES facilities. JCL is usually written by programmers or computer operators, but there are many departmental users who write their own. Unlike programming languages that have some recognizable order, JCL is a cryptic language where commas (or the absence of commas) can cause specific processing to occur. Whenever the JCL is incorrectly written, errors can happen. MVS does not see them as errors because it does only what was requested. People see them as errors because something happened that was different from what was intended. For an example of JCL, see Figure 1.2. It shows a job with three steps for a sample payroll. JCL statements are usually identified by the appearance of two slash marks (//) in the leftmost positions.

```
1. //PAYWK103 JOB  (FINDEPT,5,20,,9999),'BIWEEKLY PAY',
   //       REGION=800K,CLASS=P
2. //JOBLIB    DD      DSN=FINANCE.PGMLIB,DISP=SHR
3. //PAY1      EXEC    SORTPROC,PROG=PAYSORT
4. //EMPFILE   DD      DSN=FINANCE.EMPLOYEE.FILE,DISP=SHR
5. //SORTFIL   DD      DSN=&&SORTED,DISP=(,PASS),UNIT=SYSDA,
   //       SPACE=(TRK,(20,10),RLSE),DCB=BLKSIZE=22140
6. //ERRORS    DD      SYSOUT=*
   //PAY2      EXEC PGM=CALC,COND=(0,LT)
   //INFILE    DD      DSN=&&SORTED,DISP=(OLD,DELETE)
   //NEWFILE   DD      DSN=&&TEMP,DISP=(NEW,PASS),UNIT=SYSDA,
   //       SPACE=(CYL,10),DCB=BLKSIZE=22140
   //PAY3      EXEC PGM=PAYRPT,COND=(0,LT)
   //PAYFIL    DD      DSN=&&TEMP,DISP=OLD
   //REGISTR   DD      SYSOUT=A
   //CHECKS    DD      SYSOUT=(F,CHEK)
7. //
```

Figure 1.2. Example of JCL.

You may be wondering, "Why does JCL use // in the first two positions?" Good question. As you will come to realize, MVS evolved; it was not originally in its current state. In the beginning (I like that phrase), all computer input data was on punched cards, each containing 80 characters of information. This was still true when the earliest versions of MVS (called OS) emerged. Since many data files were on punched cards, there was a need to easily identify job control statements from other punched cards. Someone (or a committee) decided that slash marks in the first two positions were sufficiently unusual to allow the operating system to distinguish JCL punched cards from data punched cards. Now, in the 1990s (although punched cards are almost extinct), MVS still uses 80-character data structures for all of its commands. (Note: Most programming languages still follow this custom, using an 80-character data structure for program instructions.)

No, you are not expected to learn JCL in this book. (Whew!) Figure 1.2 just gives you an example of what it looks like. Every job will vary considerably from this, but all share the same look. I numbered several of the statements to explain the concepts to you.

Statement 1 is a JOB statement, identifying to MVS that all following JCL statements (until statement 7) are to be processed as one logical unit. The name that will be used when communicating to the computer operator and any accounting processes will be PAYWK103. The department being charged for this job has the code FINDEPT. As you might imagine, the choice of terms and codes for a company or department needs to be well documented and communicated.

Statement 3 (I'll explain statement 2 in Chapter 3) identifies to MVS the name of the program to use for the first step. MVS will give control of the computer to the named program if it can be located.

Statements 4 through 6 identify the data files (the JCL term for a file is *dataset*) that will be used in the first step. MVS locates these files for the named program.

Statement 7, by having nothing coded except the two slash marks, identifies to MVS that this marks the end of the job, PAYWK103.

The names used in Figure 1.2 are only examples. When MVS software is installed on a computer, the company's programmers who support MVS (known as *systems programmers*) define what names will be used at the company to represent such items as storage devices or printer forms. The application programmers who write the application programs (such as payroll) decide what names will be used to identify their programs and files. The selected names usually influence the process by which a data center keeps track of (or charges for) computer usage. Selected names for programs and files are also

8 THE MVS PRIMER

important to ensure proper integrity and security, a service usually performed by a data management or security department. Obviously, standards are needed for a large data center to function smoothly. JCL that works at one data center may not work at another. At better data centers, the standards are well documented and readily available to help new users with the computer. Less effective data centers also have standards but, because they may not be documented, learning them requires persistence.

In addition to isolating a series of steps that represent a function, JCL also provides various controls that help the operations personnel manage jobs. This varies from providing accounting information and statistics for a job to controls that address the flow of steps within a job. Since JCL is beyond this book, I suggest you consider another QED book, *MVS/JCL: Mastering Job Control Language* (Chapter 7), if you want to learn JCL. In many companies, there is a separate career path for JCL specialists, but programmers and other computer users will always need a good working knowledge of this intricate and interesting computer language.

1.1.3. System flowcharts

System flowcharts are usually prepared for each job to provide some visual recognition of the processes. (Note: A system flowchart is *not* a program flowchart. System flowcharts represent *what* data is being processed and *when* (what sequence). A program flowchart represents *how* the data is processed, showing a logical flow within a program.). For an example of a system flowchart that complements the JCL in Figure 1.2, see Figure 1.3, which only displays the concept. Usually, a system flowchart contains enough information so the people who use the system (the payroll department personnel, in our example) can understand it.

System flowcharts are useful because they document where various reports are produced and identify where certain processes occur. In Figure 1.3, datasets are represented in double lines.

FUNCTIONS OF MVS

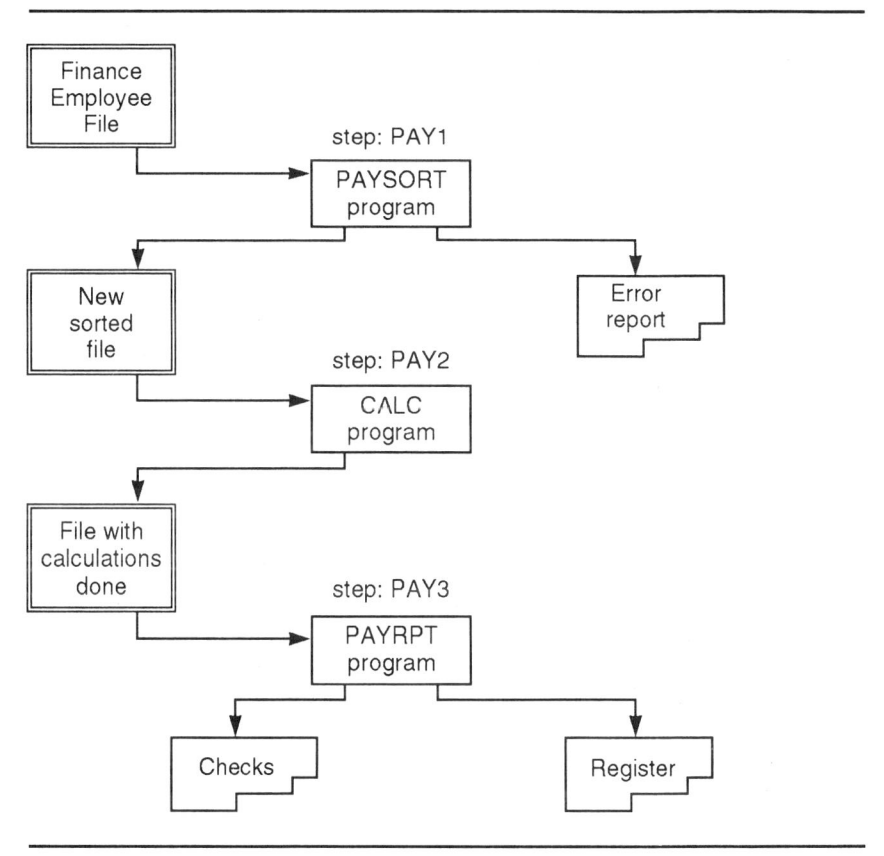

Figure 1.3. Sample system flowchart.

SECTION REVIEW

Some people feel that JCL is the worst feature of MVS because it is so complex. Actually, JCL gives MVS its strength. By providing many complex options and features, JCL ensures that what MVS does correctly once can be done correctly every time that same JCL is used. As you progress through this book, always look for the JCL aspect. It is almost always a factor, whether for batch operations or for online transactions. Job management is a key factor for any centrally administered data center, because it ensures the work done for each department is consistent, controlled, and documented. From my experience, of all the skills used and taught at MVS data centers, JCL is the least understood and the least taught. I believe there is a correlation there. If you aspire to be an MVS processing expert at your company, start by developing a strong knowledge of JCL.

Note: While you will find that I recommend several QED books in this text to assist you, my primary goal is to encourage you to invest in your own personal reference library of books. Any suggestions I make are because, having read the book, I feel it can be a quality addition to a personal library. Few things frustrate me more than encountering programmers who depend solely on their employer for supplying reference material. To do so compromises the programmers' careers. It is not uncommon for companies to (unwisely) buy only one copy of each needed IBM reference manual and then lock it into a nonmovable binder. If you must share a manual with several hundred other programmers, you can't be productive. Survival becomes the goal. (This practice, by the way, is not very cost-effective. Every time a programmer wastes 30 minutes of work time searching for information, the price of the needed book is paid for.)

1.2. TASK MANAGEMENT

Job management has always been a part of computer operations, except that it may have been done manually or more easily with earlier systems. That isn't true for task management, which brings a major cost-efficiency factor to MVS systems. *Task management* is the function of allowing a variety of different jobs to share the CPU concurrently.

Consider a large company with many departments, each requiring that many different jobs be processed throughout the day, week, or month. Imagine that the company also has several hundred terminals accessing the computer at the same time. Through its task management facilities, MVS ensures that all these units of work, while being separately controlled by job management, receive appropriate CPU access to achieve processing objectives. Task management also schedules use of equipment that is needed by more than one job, such as tape drives. This prevents two different jobs from attempting to use a device that cannot be shared. Usually (because the speed of modern computers is so fast) there is no visually apparent delay as MVS transfers access to the CPU from job to job.

When CPU access is switched among many jobs, you might think all jobs must be delayed (much as several persons would be delayed if they were sharing a single pencil). But a better comparison would be where many persons shared the same pencil *sharpener*, an important resource but one that isn't in constant use. MVS takes advantage of the fact that users of any computer resource use it only occasionally, at most.

What allows MVS to share the use of critical resources with little impact on the total time needed to accomplish a unit of work is the difference in the resources' processing speeds. See Figure 1.4 for an example of how several tasks might compete for the CPU. The delay that each task experiences is caused by the wait for other services, such as a reply from a terminal, completion of an I/O request, or possibly a service by a computer operator (such as locating a reel of tape and mounting it on a tape drive). Consider these two theoretical examples.

Person at terminal:

1. Talks to customer on telephone to get information about a change of address. *30 seconds*
2. Types in customer number. *5 seconds*
3. Computer locates customer data.
   - MVS gives control to transaction. *1/100 second*
   - Transaction program reads data from terminal screen and requests that MVS make the customer record available. *1/50 second*
   - MVS issues I/O to storage device to read record. *1/100 second*

- Transaction *waits* until data is read into memory and MVS gives control of the CPU back to the transaction.
  1/2 second
- Transaction formats terminal response and writes it to operator's terminal. *1/50 second*

TOTAL: *0.56 second*

4. Terminal operator confirms to customer that change of address has been recorded. *15 seconds*

Batch job updating a database:

1. Program in a job step requests that MVS locate the next employee record. *1/100 second*

2. MVS issues I/O to storage device. *1/100 second*

3. While this program waits, MVS gives control of the CPU to another program that may have similar processing. When data has been read for this program, MVS returns control of the CPU back to the program. *1/2 second*

4. Program does calculations on employee data for gross pay and deductions. *1/50 second*

5. Program requests that MVS write the updated data record back to the file. *1/100 second*

6. MVS issues I/O to storage device. *1/100 second*

7. Program waits again while I/O takes place and CPU is being used by other programs. *1/4 second*

8. MVS returns control to program, which then repeats step 1, above.

In the two examples, the times are not realistic, as computers operate in much smaller fractions of a second. Still, this demonstrates that the person or program is involved in processes other than using the CPU. In the second example, the (relatively) long wait time for I/O to take place is because the disk and tape storage devices have components that physically

TASKS	Allocation of CPU by MVS to each task
Person at terminal	X X X
Database update	X X X
Payroll program	X X X
Inventory report	X X X
	Time blocks with no CPU use represent excess capacity, i.e., all programs are running at their maximum speed.

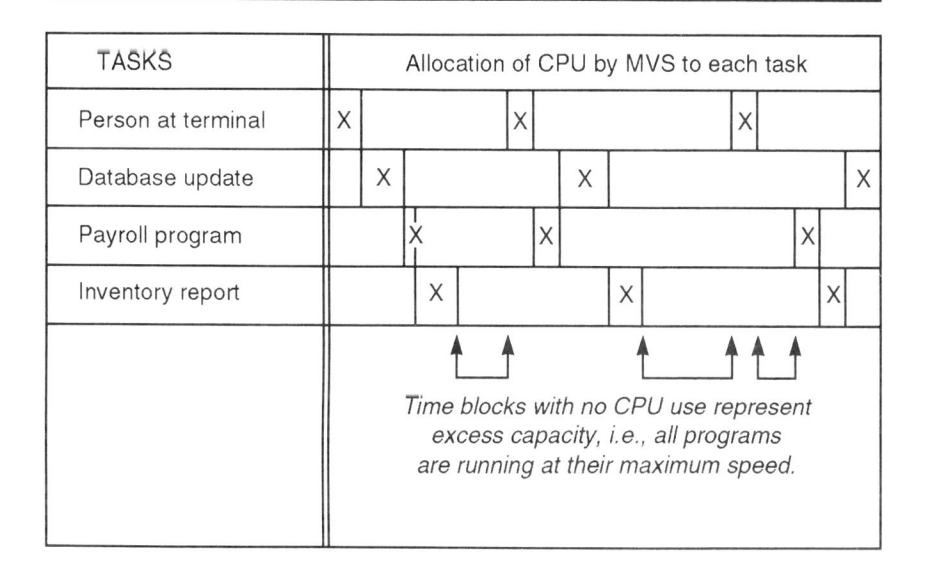

Figure 1.4. Example of multiple tasks sharing CPU.

move. This movement of the tape or the disk access arm is so much slower than the CPU speed that MVS takes advantage of the delay by immediately giving control of the CPU to a job that is *not* still waiting for I/O requests to be completed. Since the affected programs would need to wait anyway, the effect on elapsed time is often nonexistent or is negligible.

Sometimes, however, the computer becomes overloaded, each job in the system experiences delays in processing because there are too many jobs competing for the CPU. For example, when a CPU-intensive task is added to the tasks shown in Figure 1.4 (see Figure 1.5), all tasks have less access to the CPU. Another example would be with large online systems. Terminal users experience what is known as *poor response time* during those peak periods when the computer is receiving the most demand for its services. MVS attempts to alleviate this problem by giving different priorities to different tasks, thereby ensuring that functions such as online transactions receive a high priority.

14 THE MVS PRIMER

TASKS	Allocation of CPU by MVS to each task
Person at terminal	X X
Database update	X X
Payroll program	X X
Inventory report	X X
Actuarial formula	X X
	Now, with an added task that uses lots of calculations, the CPU is overscheduled, causing delays in all processing.

Figure 1.5. Example of overloaded CPU.

Because task management is a key factor in a company's efficient use of its computer(s), most large companies have employees whose primary function is to monitor this process. This is done by checking various MVS statistics during the day and making periodic forecasts to upper management on projected requirements for additional computing power (often referred to as *computing capacity*).

SECTION REVIEW

Task management is transparent to the computer user while (part of) job management is not. MVS balances work across available computing resources by task management. The balancing of multiple jobs' access to the CPU is often referred to as *multiprogramming*. MVS's task management is a major factor in making a large data center cost-effective for corporate use, allowing all users to concurrently access and share the CPU and data files.

1.3. DATA MANAGEMENT

Data management is an MVS function that is often taken for granted — especially by people who work with MVS-controlled computers. Some other computer operating systems possess much less data management, requiring more involvement by the person who uses the computer. So, what is *data management*? It is the process of organizing data for retrieval and update, and storing it in such a fashion that the programmer or operator doesn't need to know many of the technical specifics. Data management addresses such issues as accessing data in different file structures, physical access to the data, and locating the data. I will address each issue separately. Because data management concepts are somewhat more visible to MVS users, this topic may be more complex than my discussions of job management and task management. Remember as you read this information that, although it is complex, it is a service performed by MVS, and the programmer does not need either to know or understand any of it. Structuring the data management portion of MVS is yet another function performed by a company's systems programmers. Also, MVS locates and accesses executable programs through a route different from the one it uses to locate and access data files. More on that later.

1.3.1. Access methods

An *access method* is a collection of MVS programs that read, write, and update data files in a particular file structure. MVS provides different access methods for different file structures, often without even requiring that the programmer be aware of it. These access methods free the programmer from the time-consuming process of writing complex code to manipulate tape reels, intercept data errors, check for location of control fields on disk devices, and other technical details.

While access methods existed to a degree before MVS, they are more comprehensive in their services today. (Chapter 2 will review what some of these early processes were and the impact they had on the programming process.) Programmers can now write programs with little or no knowledge of the types of data storage devices that a data center uses. This allows programs to be moved easily from one environment to another and also allows the data center staff to move data files from one storage device to another more easily.

Coupled with task management, MVS's access methods provide still other critical services, this time not for a specific program but to protect the data within the data center environment itself. For example, one service of VSAM (Virtual Storage Access Method, pronounced *vee-sam*) is to prevent other programs from accessing a data record while another program is updating the record. This is a factor of data integrity where many tasks might want to access a common record.

Because MVS is used in large mainframe computers, many major corporations rely on MVS to control their mission-critical applications. It was the need to allow more extensive control of, and access to, corporate data that caused IBM to develop two major software components that far exceed the definition of *access method*. Those components are IMS (Information Management System) and DB2 (DATABASE 2). Although these components aren't discussed in detail until Chapter 3, I mention them here because these software components provide extensive structural opportunities for the organization and manipulation of data files. Technically, these are not access methods, because they in turn use various access methods to accomplish their goal. IMS and DB2 both provide extensive data security features.

What these two software components provide is a layered approach to data, separating various parts of the process into separately managed components. Here are two examples of layered structures.

Earlier, I encouraged you to be sensitive to the possibility of a JCL element in any topic. Because access methods define data and programs, JCL is a major part of bringing all these components together for MVS's use. For example, it is through JCL that MVS incorporates IMS into a job, locates the information

FUNCTIONS OF MVS 17

Normal MVS application
(for sequential and simple structures)

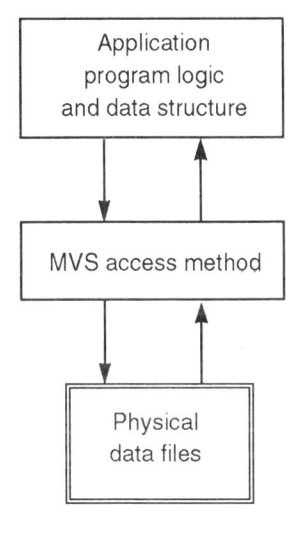

```
┌─────────────────────┐
│    Application      │
│   program logic     │
│ and data structure  │
└─────────────────────┘
          ↕
┌─────────────────────┐
│  MVS access method  │
└─────────────────────┘
          ↕
┌─────────────────────┐
│      Physical       │
│     data files      │
└─────────────────────┘
```

MVS application with IMS or DB2
(for complex data structures)

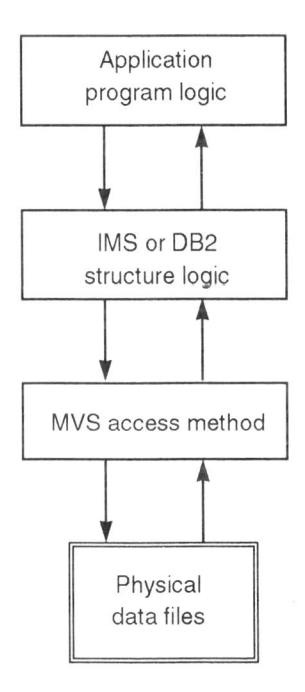

```
┌─────────────────────┐
│    Application      │
│   program logic     │
└─────────────────────┘
          ↕
┌─────────────────────┐
│    IMS or DB2       │
│   structure logic   │
└─────────────────────┘
          ↕
┌─────────────────────┐
│  MVS access method  │
└─────────────────────┘
          ↕
┌─────────────────────┐
│      Physical       │
│     data files      │
└─────────────────────┘
```

on the appropriate data structures, and locates the physical file on a particular storage device.

In the next topic, you will see an additional function of access methods, that of providing programmed instructions to the hardware components of the computer system. The process of managing data in the ever-expanding MVS corporate data centers would be impossible without access methods.

1.3.2. Handling the I/O

The next issue to address is the physical access to the data. Without MVS, this is a very technical and complex concern. To understand that, let's quickly review a simple (and abbreviated) conceptual computer configuration, shown in Figure 1.6.

18 THE MVS PRIMER

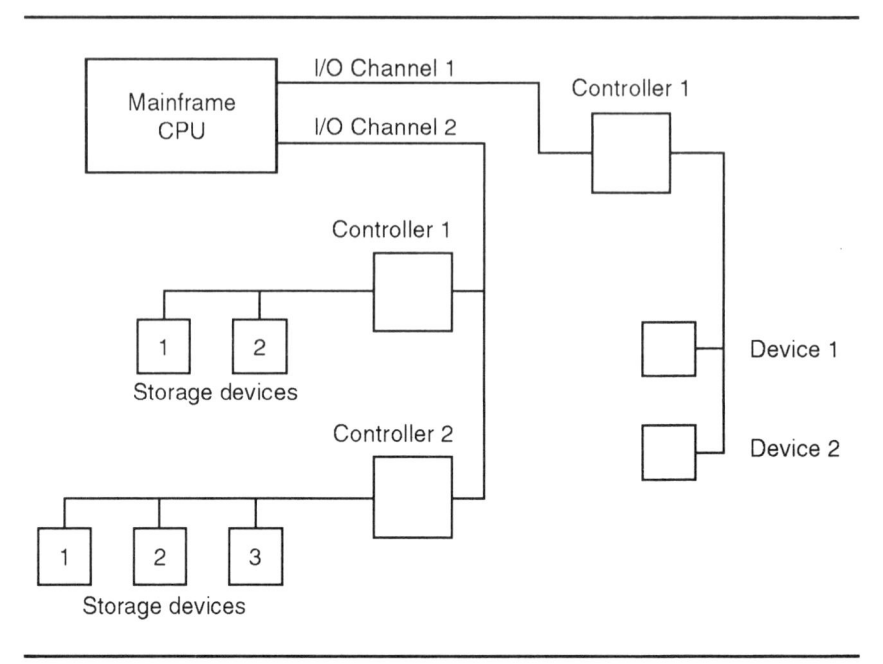

Figure 1.6. Sample computer configuration.

In Figure 1.6, the computer has two paths to data. These are called *I/O channels*. They attach to the specific data storage devices through devices called *controllers*. This structured approach is similar to a corporate organizational chart and accomplishes a similar function: delegating authority to the appropriate level. All the boxes on the chart have varying degrees of programmed capability. While the I/O channels appear to be simple cables or wires such as you might use to connect speakers to a stereo, that is not the case. The I/O channels are sophisticated, special-purpose, programmable computers in their own right. Assuming a data file has been previously located, here is a conceptual example of what occurs during an I/O request. The concepts reviewed here also relate to the earlier topic on task management.

Steps in locating a device:

1. The access method creates and gives a multistep program to the I/O channel to

- locate the device
- set the read/write arm if DASD (Direct Access Storage Device)
- wait for the disk to rotate under the read/write mechanism
- initiate a read
- wait for the read to complete
- check for data errors and reread if necessary

2. The I/O channel, being a computer separate from the mainframe computer, now proceeds independently to execute the program. The address of the data file is constructed much as you might construct addresses for a large apartment complex. You would probably identify buildings by numbers, floors by numbers, and rooms by numbers. Anyone with the three numbers could then locate any apartment throughout the complex. MVS works in a similar fashion (i.e., we don't need a rocket scientist to figure this out). By knowing the channel number, the controller number, and the device number, the I/O channel locates the device.

I just led you through a complicated process that required detailed knowledge of the physical computer configuration and, so far, all you've located is the device — but not the desired data. Now that the device is located, let's pause to review a typical device to give you an appreciation of what lies ahead. A current IBM storage device is the model 3380 disk drive. One unit of this type device contains 1.9 billion bytes of data. The data is physically organized into 15 stacked, rotating platters (my term, not IBM's), each with over 2,600 recording tracks. Each track can contain over 47,000 bytes of data. Data on the track may have identifying control records to further isolate and identify data records. Similar to the example of channels and controllers, each track has a number and each platter has a number. By combining the two, a specific track among the 2,600 tracks can be located — assuming that you know which track has the desired data.

20 THE MVS PRIMER

While some operating systems require that people in the organization keep manual records of which tracks are used for each dataset, MVS keeps it simple (although often with unappreciated — and misunderstood — planning and assistance from the installation's systems programmers). MVS does its magic by storing a table of contents for each disk device on the device itself. (Although I used the term *magic* in the previous sentence, my goal in writing this book is to remove the magic. As long as you believe that illusion is involved, or just do not grasp the underlying processes that precede what you observe, you will not understand a process.)

How MVS manages data on a device is an example of much of MVS's power — preplanning. By preplanning various processes in an MVS data center, users of the data center enjoy improved personal productivity. Let's review the table of contents feature that was mentioned above.

When a new DASD (Direct Access Storage Device, pronounced *dazz-dee*) is installed in an MVS computer configuration, it is not just uncrated and plugged into an outlet on the controller. Instead, systems programmers execute MVS utility programs that format the device, assign a unique number to it, and establish a table of contents dataset of the desired size (because the table of contents is a dataset, it requires tracks for its own use). For example, if the DASD is to be used by programmers to store small work files, the systems programmers will establish a large table of contents so it can contain information on all the anticipated datasets that the DASD may contain. Although the table of contents contains various technical information, for our purposes it is sufficient to know that the table of contents may contain the following items for each file on the DASD:

- A dataset name, up to 44 characters long. This makes it easier for an installation to devise standards for names that are meaningful to the users of the system.
- The track where the first record is located
- The size of the physical record and the size of the logical record

- The format of the record, for example, variable length or fixed length

This table of contents is called the *volume table of contents* (abbreviated as VTOC and pronounced *vee-tock*). *Volume* is a commonly used MVS term that refers to any uniquely addressable storage device, whether it is a disk drive or a reel of tape (NOT a tape drive, which cannot store data itself). The *unique number* mentioned above is referred to as a *volume serial number* (often abbreviated by programmers and operators to VOLSER (pronounced *voll-sear*) and capitalized in recognition of the similar JCL term). Every DASD has a volume serial number, and every DASD has a VTOC. (Did you remember to pronounce those acronyms instead of spelling them?) Since the VTOC contains the names of the datasets on the device, that is all you need to know for the access method to locate the dataset, once it has located the device.

1.3.3. Using the catalog

Let's review what we've covered here. First, the access method can locate the device once it knows the channel number, controller number, and device number. It can locate the tracks for the dataset on the device by using the dataset name to compare with entries in the VTOC. The user will know the dataset name, so we don't have to figure out the track location. But what about the channel, controller, and device numbers? Do you need to know those, too? In a word, no. The final feature to help us is the MVS catalog facility.

Like the VTOC, the MVS catalog achieves its goals through preplanning. Systems programmers set it/them up prior to use. Corporate naming standards come into play here as the catalogs can be constructed into a hierarchy. The catalog, like the VTOC, is organized by dataset name, and you guessed it the catalog contains the device information. (Actually, the catalog may sometimes point to another catalog, which may then contain the device information.) Let's put it all together in a conceptual example. Look at Figure 1.7.

22 THE MVS PRIMER

JCL statement: //PAYMAST DD DSNAME=FINANCE.PAYROLL.WEEKLY,...

step 1

Device: 112
master catalog

ADMIN	...
FINANCE	221
HUMANRES	...
MIS	...
.	
.	

step 2

Device: 221
user catalog

ACCTNG.LEDGER	...
ACCTNG.JOURNAL	...
PAYROLL.MONTHLY	...
PAYROLL.WEEKLY	224
.	
.	

step 3

Device: 224
VTOC

AUDIT.REPORT	...
FINANCE.PAYROLL.WEEKLY	track addr
.	
.	

step 4

FINANCE.PAYROLL.WEEKLY

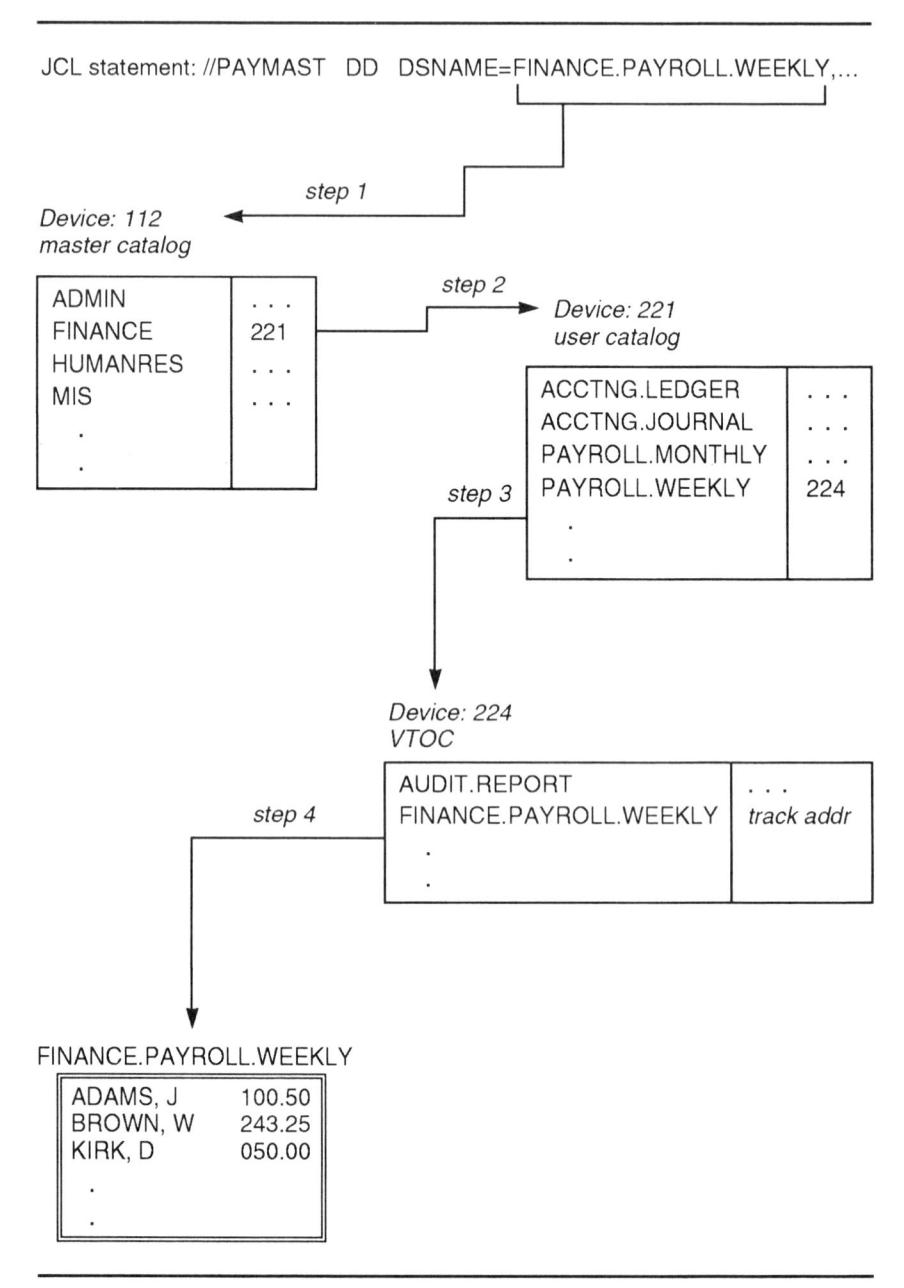

ADAMS, J	100.50
BROWN, W	243.25
KIRK, D	050.00
.	
.	

Figure 1.7. Sample catalog and VTOC structure.

In Figure 1.7, the top of the figure is a JCL statement that defines the name of a dataset, in this example FINANCE. PAYROLL.WEEKLY. (MVS allows periods to be in dataset names to allow hierarchy features. In our example, you should assume this company has decided that department names will be the highest level of the hierarchy.) The programmer enjoys freedom from this issue, which could change from time to time, by only referencing the term PAYMAST (on top line in Figure 1.7) in computer programs. This is referred to as *device-independence*, as MVS separates data files from the references to them within programs.

Using the dataset name from the JCL at the top of Figure 1.7, MVS first searches its system catalog, which was predefined by the systems programmers. There it finds an entry for the highest entry, FINANCE, which contains a device address of another catalog. Using the device address (channel 1, controller 1, device 2), the second step by MVS is to read the catalog on that device to locate additional information. There, it finds the full dataset name information and another device address. The third step is to read the VTOC on device 224. There it finds the track address where the desired dataset begins. All this is done by MVS *before* the access method attempts to use the file. Since the access method keeps the information that was provided by MVS, these steps need to be done only once for each file to be processed by any given program.

SECTION REVIEW

Data management was an involved topic, the most thorough so far. That is because the need to manage data introduces you to the computer configuration, the program libraries, and some of the functions of JCL. Although none of the information covered is necessary for survival, all of it can help you if you become involved in the use of JCL or datasets. You probably noticed that I sneaked some new words into your vocabulary. You are probably reading this book because you work at a company that uses MVS and will encounter people each day who might use such terms. At the end of the chapter you will find a review of terms.

24 THE MVS PRIMER

This is an ideal place to pause and mentally review the functions and components of job management, task management, and data management. If you feel comfortable with their contribution to a large corporate data center, even if you don't recall all the terminology, you're ready to continue with the next topic.

1.4. ENVIRONMENT CONTROL

I've already covered the major components of MVS, but you are probably exposed also to what I refer to as *environment control elements* (my term, not IBM's), components that may not be at your company but probably are. These components might not be technically part of MVS, but they exist only in the MVS environment.

1.4.1. Telecommunications and transaction systems

Earlier, I discussed access methods, possibly giving the impression that access methods were only for data files. Actually, access methods are used for every I/O from MVS. Telecommunications, the process of transmitting and receiving data from remote terminals, whether within the computer center or miles away, is no different. For this, MVS has the Virtual Telecommunications Access Method (VTAM). Although this does the work, most companies do not ask their programmers to write programs to use VTAM. This is because the complexity of developing software for online systems, coupled with the importance of online systems to companies, makes the risk too great. Instead, most companies install separate IBM transaction-management software for this function because it has already been widely tested, it is well documented, it is supported by IBM, it uses VTAM efficiently, and it lets the company's programmers focus their attention on the business application instead of on the mechanics of transmitting and receiving to a terminal. (Note: A *transaction* is a term that generally means a specific function that is performed from an online terminal. Security is often enforced at a transaction level, letting one

FUNCTIONS OF MVS   25

employee execute the transaction that changes a customer's address on the database but not the transaction that changes the customer's credit limit.)

The two software components that are used the most for managing online transactions are CICS (for Customer Information Control System, pronounced *kicks*) and IMS/DC (Information Management System/Data Communications, always spelled out and not pronounced). (Note: Earlier, I referred to IMS. IMS/DC is a subset of the IMS environment.) These components will receive more attention in Chapters 3 and 4, but each is too complex to receive a thorough review in this book. If you are able to use these terms correctly in conversation, I will consider the coverage in this book a success. (If you want to gain more knowledge of these two software components, I suggest you check out the books listed in Chapter 7.) The logical view of a given interaction with a terminal is shown below. This structure isolates terminal management and many performance issues from the application, providing better control and monitoring than would otherwise be true.

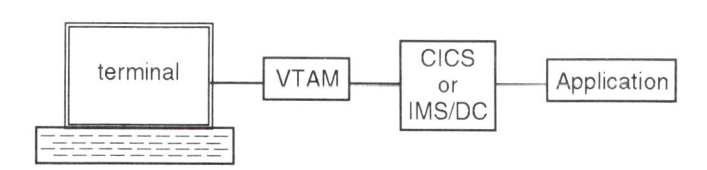

```
[terminal] -- [VTAM] -- [CICS or IMS/DC] -- [Application]
```

Both products (CICS and IMS/DC) provide services to simplify the programmer's task and also provide services for MVS, helping to balance the workload among the many terminals that may be using the computer. Both are software environments that require centralized control and administration and are not controllable by terminal users or programmers (other than use of their personal terminal). How is the control and administration accomplished? With JCL, of course. Major components of MVS that touch all users are controlled by operators in the data center who submit special JCL to MVS at the

26 THE MVS PRIMER

beginning of the day or week, depending on the company's work schedule. Until the operators *bring up* the CICS or IMS/DC software, the terminals are inoperative. Likewise, if the operators *shut down* the system, the terminals return to inoperative status. See Figure 1.8 for a conceptual view of the structure.

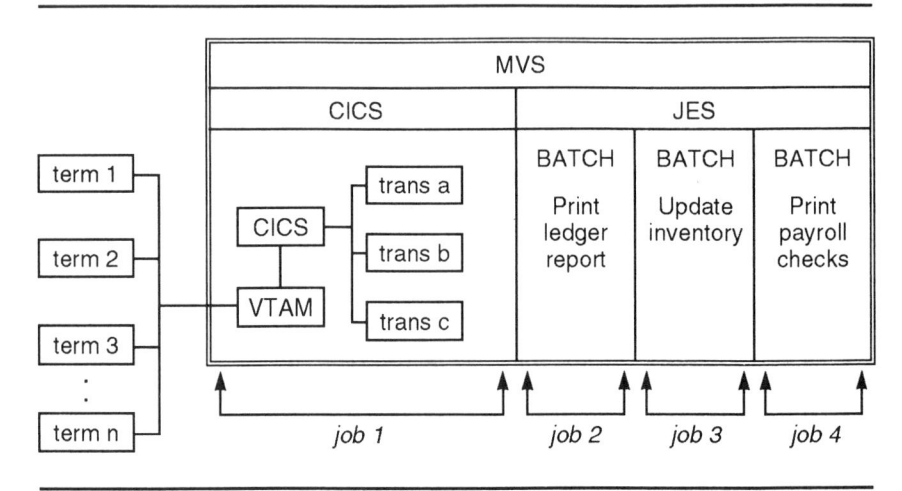

Figure 1.8. Conceptual telecommunications view.

In Figure 1.8, the mainframe environment is represented by the double-lined box. In the example, I used CICS, but this is *not* a technical view of that system (IMS/DC would appear similar). It is a conceptual view of the environment showing that, at this point in time, MVS is coordinating four jobs. Three of the jobs are batch, as discussed previously in job management and task management. The first *job* (job 1) is not really a job as I defined it previously but a system task initiated by a computer operator. (A system task is a set of specialized JCL that can only be submitted to MVS by authorized operators, not by programmers.) In our example, CICS is coordinating three separate transaction programs with an unknown number of terminals.

Now, let's build on the knowledge you've gained so far and draw some observations. Notice that MVS only sees four jobs. It does *not* see that many terminals are interacting with the transaction programs. Only CICS sees that (concepts represented here would also be true for IMS/DC). From our discussion on task management, you know that MVS keeps each job separate from the others. From that, you can deduce that an error in job 4 (print payroll checks) would not affect the other jobs. However, look at job 1. If CICS had a major catastrophic program error, there is a good possibility that all three transactions would stop and that all the terminals would cease functioning.

This isolation of function is a strength of MVS, not a weakness. By delegating transaction management to a software component such as CICS, MVS can concentrate on a bigger picture, the whole data center operation. CICS, in turn, manages transactions and terminals. So, if one of the transaction programs had an error, CICS would stop the transaction and let the others continue to function.

This separation of accountability also provides for many career paths in an MVS data center. In the previous example, a CICS specialist would be authorized to add or change terminals, authorize new or modified applications, and do other performance and administrative functions. By having specialists for each major function, it is easier to provide help or assistance when a terminal or transaction malfunctions.

If you've ever used CICS or IMS/DC, you probably noticed that you must go through two steps to reach the transaction you want. First, you log onto the environment software. This is necessary so that CICS or IMS/DC will know who you are and can validate any security or other authority you might have. Second, you log onto the desired transaction. Since you first completed step 1, the system can confirm that you are authorized to use the transaction and establishes a connection between your terminal and the transaction program. (For example, although you might be authorized to use a computer terminal, you might not be authorized to use the transaction that changes an employee's salary.)

28 THE MVS PRIMER

Since CICS and IMS/DC were introduced years ago, they have grown considerably in the services they provide. These services include the ability to recover from serious problems, provide logs of transaction activity, change priorities of different services, and provide varying degrees of data protection. For more detailed information on these systems, see Chapter 7 for information on other publications.

1.4.2. Time-sharing services

This topic is very similar to the previous one but differs in important aspects. One of the services of MVS is the ability to allow multiple terminals to share direct access to the power and capability of MVS. Unlike transaction systems where the application program controls what functions a terminal user can have, time sharing is a facility whereby the terminal user is given a significant degree of authority. This authority allows time-sharing users to execute programs of their choice, create and submit JCL to MVS, and use a rich array of software services to create and modify application programs. Clearly, time-sharing users are those persons at a company with the necessary knowledge to create and execute their own computer programs.

Time sharing was first offered on MVS (known as OS at that time, for Operating System, and pronounced *oh-ess*) in the early 1970s. At that time, it was an optional, extra-cost, software product and was known as TSO (Time Sharing Option). The name stuck. TSO it was and TSO it still is, even though it is no longer an option (also, TSO has never been pronounced as a word, unusual for IBM software). As it did with CICS and IMS/DC, IBM packages TSO as a separate, delegated environment so MVS can control it as an element within the system. A conceptual view of TSO would be very similar to that shown in Figure 1.8. (Note: CICS, IMS/DC, and TSO are not mutually exclusive. It is not uncommon to find all three operating concurrently at an MVS data center. More on this in Chapters 3 and 4.)

While transaction systems can support an almost unlimited number of terminals, time sharing creates such a load on MVS that companies usually put limits and restrictions on which persons may use it. Normally, programmers use this facility to build and test programs along with computer-literate end users who write their own reports or queries. Also, since TSO was developed in the early 1970s, many of its native features are archaic today. To make the system easier to use, IBM provides a software product called ISPF (Interactive Structured Programming Facility) to let users access menus to use TSO's power. Some people do programming in the native TSO command language, and these programs are called CLISTs (Command Lists). At most sites, programmers do not need to master this language and use CLISTs that were developed for shop-wide use. Another language that has recently emerged for TSO programming is REXX (Restructured Extended Executor). (More information will be presented on these topics in Chapters 3, 4, and 5. You will also find several books listed in Chapter 7 that will help you master any of these software environments.)

There are implications here for the user of these online services. To use these software components, you may find that you need many passwords, one for CICS, one for IMS/DC, one for TSO, and possibly one for each of the CICS and IMS/DC transactions that you are authorized to use. Normally, having this many passwords (or having no passwords) is indicative that the data center has yet to develop a strategy for computer security.

1.4.3. Security

Security is optional with MVS, which is as it should be. A data center must make decisions on what should be secure and what should not. Life is easier if one identifies what must be secured instead of identifying what is not. The MVS product that provides system-wide security (as opposed to application-specific security or terminal security) is RACF (Resource Access Control Facility, pronounced *rack off*). A strength of RACF is that it is administered by people. If something goes wrong, it can usually be quickly corrected. If RACF is installed at a data center, MVS lets it validate every attempt to access data or programs.

When a violation is detected, RACF logs the event for review by the security administrator at the data center. It can also send messages to the terminal users, notifying them of their infractions.

Another feature of RACF is the ability to allow some persons to access specific data and refuse access to others. Consider the situation where a team of programmers is working on the payroll system. They must have some degree of access to certain datasets to check out and correct program errors, even though they are not employees of the payroll unit. Likewise, employees in the payroll unit might have total access to all such data. All other company employees should, obviously, not have such access.

The presence of RACF on the computer you use should not cause you to feel that you aren't trusted or that you should be afraid to do your assigned job. At most installations, the majority of reported infractions by RACF are accidental. If you ever receive such a warning, look at it as an opportunity to review what authority you have and what you may and may not access. RACF provides a great degree of security to a data center and provides services to protect your data as well as that of others.

1.4.4. Accounting and monitoring

Because accounting and monitoring functions meet requirements particular to each data center, MVS does not provide standardized reports of computer activity. It does something better. MVS provides a log of system activity complete with detailed computer use statistics. From this data file, installation programmers usually prepare reports that are unique to the installation. One benefit of such data is the ability to charge user departments for services received. These charges are usually administered by a clerical unit at the data center, but some companies have created online reports for this function.

For these reasons, you should not assume that you are (or are not) charged for services at an MVS data center. Nor should you make assumptions on which resources are billed and which are not. This varies from company to company. One company may charge for CPU time, another for the number of transactions processed, another for the number of DASD tracks used, and another for some combination of them all. To encourage users to use the computer during off-peak work hours, some companies offer discounts if work is done after normal work hours. (Note: I've seen entire programming teams come to work at midnight to lower the cost of a project and — more important — to receive better response time on rush projects.)

Every time you submit JCL or log onto an MVS system, you should assume that MVS is tracking your activities and logging your resource use. Use the resources wisely and sensitively.

SECTION REVIEW

We covered several of the highly visible aspects of MVS and most of those from which new careers have formed. TSO, CICS, IMS, DB2, and RACF all require support from specially trained personnel. Likewise, the increased complexity of charging for services and the need for resource management have created specialty positions for the administration and monitoring of these features.

CHAPTER REVIEW

This chapter exposed you to more of MVS than many active MVS users receive throughout their career. We will review many of these terms further in the book. For now, I wanted to introduce their basic roles in MVS. You could stop reading the book at this point and be comfortable in your casual interaction with MVS, in cocktail party conversations about MVS (only systems programmers would enjoy discussing this topic at a party — but that doesn't mean they don't know how to enjoy a party), or in managing people who work in an MVS data center. I encourage you to continue onward for better understanding, not only of MVS mechanics but of the benefits of some of the components I've briefly mentioned, and for insight into the skills needed in a well-run MVS data center.

VOCABULARY REVIEW

Here are the main terms introduced in this chapter. When you can use each of them in a sentence, you will know you've got it. Try filling in these sample sentences.

The JCL statement that provides accounting information for the job is the _____ statement.

A _____ identifies the location of all datasets on a disk storage unit.

The two programming languages that run in TSO are _____ and _____ .

The unit within a job that executes a specific program is known as a _____ .

The entry on a DASD that has the name of all datasets on the DASD is known as the _____ .

The two most widely used transaction control systems are _____ and _____ .

Here are some of the terms used in this chapter. Can you use each of them in a sentence?

job

step

catalog

dataset

VTOC

DD

access method

IMS

DB2

TSO

DASD

CLIST

REXX

JCL

system flowchart

program flowchart

The time: Tuesday morning, 2:00 A.M.

The location: A typical programmer's bedroom

"I'm sure that marrying David wasn't the worst thing I ever did, but sometimes I wonder. That darn telephone seems to ring almost every night, just as if it owned David. When it rings, he has to get dressed and drive the 15 miles to the data center because something went "wrong" — whatever "wrong" is. Sometimes, I'd like to enjoy a life where my husband goes to bed with me and wakes up with me. That doesn't seem to be in our future, at least not now.

"I guess the phone rang about 15 minutes ago, and David must be already on the highway by now. What unnerves me is the casual way the other person on the phone says, 'Is Dave there?,' just as though it were midafternoon. Where do they *think* he is at this time of night, and why can't they be courteous enough to at least identify themselves at this late hour?

"I know I'll get over this. David doesn't like it any better than I do. Maybe it's just that the computer seems to own him, telling him when he's needed and when he isn't. I sure pray that someone at his company knows what sacrifices he makes for them. Oh, well, maybe he'll get to come home early — but probably not. Life was much simpler when he worked at that small company where they shut the computer off at quitting time. David insists that this is a better career opportunity, but what about our life together? Isn't that important, too?"

2
History of Operating Systems

Although the title of this chapter may cause you to feel that the topic is irrelevant to a modern operating system like MVS, the opposite is true. MVS evolved to meet the needs of people who used the computer. Having an awareness of how computers were operated prior to the arrival of comprehensive operating systems will help you to grasp the productivity aspects of many options that are often taken for granted. Having some knowledge of pre-MVS operating systems will also help you to appreciate better just what MVS is doing today and why it continues to grow in capability.

2.1. PREOPERATING SYSTEM WORLD

Until the late 1960s, many computers had no operating software at all. A few began to emerge in the early 1960s, but their capability was limited to a few basic functions. Let's look at a typical operation.

In many ways, these computers were appealing, primarily because they were so dependent on constant human attention. When the computer was not processing a program, it was doing nothing. Whenever any component hardware elements (such as printers and tape drives) failed to operate properly, the computer just stopped. There were no operator messages, no error

36 THE MVS PRIMER

codes, no ability to bypass the problem; it just stopped. Only by knowing how to decipher the binary codes in a set of lights on the computer console could a skilled technician coax the machine onward. A far cry from today.

When these early computers finally had a formal programming language (an assembler language), the language compile process created a complete standalone program. This program had to provide not only the application logic but also the logic for every function of the computer needed by the application. Being under total control of a single application, the computer was incapable of doing any other process until the current program was completed. Here is a typical scenario.

- A computer operator comes to work in the morning and turns on the computer, much as you might turn on the morning radio. Other than the normal electrical processes of warming up the circuitry, nothing else happens as there is no software automatically loaded.

- Next, the operator reviews the lists of what jobs are to be run that day. Each *job* is usually one or more typed pages of instructions, identifying what programs to run, in what sequence, what tapes to process, and what type of paper to put in the printer (preprinted forms, for example).

- From each job sheet, the operator goes to file cabinets, takes the program decks (punched cards), and lays them out on a work table in the order in which they are to be processed. Then the operator puts the proper paper in the printer and goes to the tape closet to locate the tape reel numbers listed on the job sheet (done manually after each running).

- After this preparatory work, the operator puts the first program card deck in the card reader and presses the LOAD button. Finally, the computer comes to life. Using preprogrammed circuitry not unlike that in a PC, the computer reads the first card of the deck and executes the first instruction on it. That's it. From that first instruction, the computer program is on its own to ensure the remaining program cards are read into memory, that the memory is cleared where necessary, that tape drives and other devices are ready, and that the operator is notified of any discrepancies. This was often referred to as a *bootstrap process* after the expression "pull yourself up by your bootstraps." As you can see, the program (and the programmer) had responsibility not only for the application logic but for the proper functioning of the computer as well.

- After the first program stops (programs didn't exactly *end*; they just stopped) the operator must put the program deck back in the file cabinet, write the new tape reel numbers on the job sheet, and then pick up the next program deck and repeat the process.

This little scenario is what I referred to in the previous chapter as a *job*: a series of processes to accomplish a business function. This completely manual process was fraught with error, it was clumsy, and it was a poor use of the operator's time. Most of all, it was so time-consuming that very few jobs were processed each day, causing the computer to be idle more often than busy.

Also, it wasn't uncommon for programmers to test programs at midnight because they had to wait until all the day's jobs had been run. Operators couldn't run the tests for them because, being new programs, there were no instructions for them. So, programmers worked days to write the programs and nights to test them. Yes, this affected their personal lives, and not for the better. The progress outlined in this book improved the work environment for programmers but, programmers must still work unusual schedules, and the programming career field still attracts a special breed of people who find the excitement of programming is worth the price. I identify with them.

SECTION REVIEW

This was a short section, primarily because there is little that happened in the early years that can relate to the large mainframe environment today. I included this background to present some of the issues that operating systems were hoped to solve.

2.2. SECOND-GENERATION MACHINES

When people discuss computers by their *generation*, they usually use the following terms:

- First generation: computers that used vacuum tubes and separately wired electrical components for circuitry.

- Second generation: computers that used magnetic cores for memory, and transistors and other solid state components for circuitry.

- Third generation: computers that use integrated microelectronics for circuitry and memory.

These definitions were pretty well set by the early 1970s. I won't even attempt to define *fourth* or *fifth generation*. The industry has been debating these terms ever since the ink dried on *third generation*. Now, the definitions I gave might be fine for an engineer, but they are useless to me and other programmers because they don't indicate any changes in programming processes or application opportunities (other than speed). Here are my definitions for the terms. The time frames for my definitions are similar to those for the previous definitions, but I allow for significant overlap:

- First generation: computers that required totally manual programming efforts, without benefit of programming languages, libraries, control programs, or other support software.

- Second generation: computers that provided the basic tools for program development and operation, recognizing that the computer and its support software were required for the computer to be used productively.

- Third generation: computers that provided integrated software and hardware for all services for which the computer can perform. I include MVS in this category although MVS has grown significantly beyond this simple definition.

Refer to Figure 2.1. While not technically correct (purists will always argue the generations of computers), this gives you the concept of what the environments were like.

Generation	Hardware	Software
First generation	Vacuum tubes	Machine language
Second generation	Transistors	Job schedulers
Third generation	Integrated circuits	Operating systems

Figure 2.1. Overview of computer generations.

The second generation had a short lifespan, but it was an interesting period of computer evolution and the period during which the foundation of computer operating systems developed. Full programming languages, libraries, support programs, and services were developed during this period and took full advantage of the limited computers of the day.

2.2.1. Programming languages

Although computer time was more costly than programmer time, the corporate focus was on ways to improve the programming process. (Yes, there was much interest in making programs more efficient, but those were short-term efforts.) Prior to programming languages, programmers spent most of their time coding machine-level instructions and doing manual arithmetic to ensure the addresses being coded were correct. As coding processes that solved a given function emerged, programmers were quick to realize the coding for these solutions should be saved and shared with other programmers. These early shared facilities were in manually controlled file cabinets, but they set the stage for future improvements. Most of all, they pointed the way to what was beneficial to programmers: simpler coding and shared facilities.

The early programming languages (such as IBM's Autocoder language) were significant productivity improvements, allowing a programmer to reference data areas by programmer-assigned names. (See Figure 2.2.) This also freed the programmer from remembering the machine-level instruction formats and from manually computing program addresses. These language processors (called *assemblers* because they assembled one machine instruction from one source statement) also relieved the programmer from the tedious task of writing the code for the bootstrap process mentioned previously. The output from the assembler was a punched card object deck that was complete in every detail for subsequent loading into the computer. The source language was referred to as *assembler language*. The term is still used to denote any machine-oriented programming language that has a one-to-one conversion to machine code. (Yes, MVS has an assembler language.)

Machine language: Add a value and move to print buffer
    A025764
    Z764225

Autocoder language: Add a value and move to print buffer
    A   AMOUNT,TOTAL
    MCS   TOTAL,TOTOUT

Figure 2.2. Example of machine language versus Autocoder language.

At a more subtle level, but more important to the future of programming languages and operating systems, was the concurrent emergence of macro-level coding facilities that provided prewritten program subsets that could be easily introduced into a program. Tape drives were the primary technology that allowed large inventories of program subsets to be accessible within a programming language, beginning the slow migration from punched cards. With this macro feature, IBM was able to provide to their customers all the code needed to control nonapplication logic functions. This was the foundation on which future access methods would be built, and it was a significant factor in improving programmer productivity and in setting the stage for standardized techniques.

For example, the first program I wrote that processed data from a reel of tape (mid-1960s) required that I write code not only for the application's logic but also in order to

- rewind the reel to the beginning.

- check for a header record to verify that it was the correct reel.
- read the physical record.
- check for a transmission error.
- in the event of an error, backspace the tape and retry five times if reading it, or skip the tape forward several inches if writing it.
- check for an end-of-file mark on the tape and rewind the tape if reading it, and send a message to the operator to mount a new tape if writing it.
- for blocked records (more than one logical record per physical record), locate and adjust index pointers to keep track of the next record to process.

While it may not be obvious, the program code to accomplish the above was more complex, more tedious, and harder to debug than the application itself. The new macro facilities eliminated the need to program (or even to understand) the processes mentioned above.

This set of code (called Input Output Control System, or IOCS) was made available to programmers in the format of pseudo-instructions. These pseudo-instructions were coded by programmers as though they were traditional computer instructions (where one coded instruction generated one machine-level instruction), allowing programmers to think of the services as part of the computer when actually they were not. These new verbs that were introduced into the programmer vocabulary were words such as OPEN, CLOSE, READ, and WRITE.

We now take such terms for granted in major programming languages because we realize that programming languages should do more than generate machine-level code for application logic. In the early 1960s, that was a new way of thinking. The programming process was starting to integrate application requirements with computer control requirements, and this step created an opportunity for IBM (and other computer manufacturers) to provide standard formats in how computer resources were used. Customers preferred then (and now) to follow a standard approach that was well understood instead of doing it differently with each application. One of those standard approaches was the management of program libraries.

2.2.2. Program libraries

Program libraries were once stacks of punched cards stored in file cabinets. The term *library* never seemed appropriate as the program files were rarely well organized. With the success of standard programming languages, IBM built on the technique of using tape drives (disk drives were available but were a rarity) to store program code for operational purposes. The first major service was to store new object programs not on punched cards but on a reel of magnetic tape. This had many benefits. Punched card storage and handling was reduced, time spent searching for program decks was eliminated, and companies could begin to develop standards on program names to control the inventories. With programming languages and program library services automated and interconnected, the computer was no longer just a piece of iron but included valuable services to improve the use of it. With the emergence of program libraries, IBM (and other vendors) began to include operating software that was always resident in the computer so the program libraries could be readily searched. These were the first operating systems.

2.2.3. Use of JCL to isolate jobs

As computer software emerged, the need to identify program object decks by name grew in importance. Since programs could now be stored on electronic media that the computer could read, there was a need to name each program. This need created the first JCL used by computers, allowing the programmer or operator to precode the name of the needed program(s) for an application and let the operating software locate the required program(s) on the reel of tape. Since the computer could run only one program at a time, this was the practical limit for most JCL in this era. This allowed an operator to place a deck of punched cards, each with the name of a program to run, in the card reader for the computer and to run each program in the deck's sequence.

HISTORY OF OPERATING SYSTEMS   43

Although primitive, this eliminated many of the procedural errors of pulling card decks from file cabinets and loading them into the computer from printed operator instruction sheets. A conceptual example of second generation is shown in Figure 2.3.

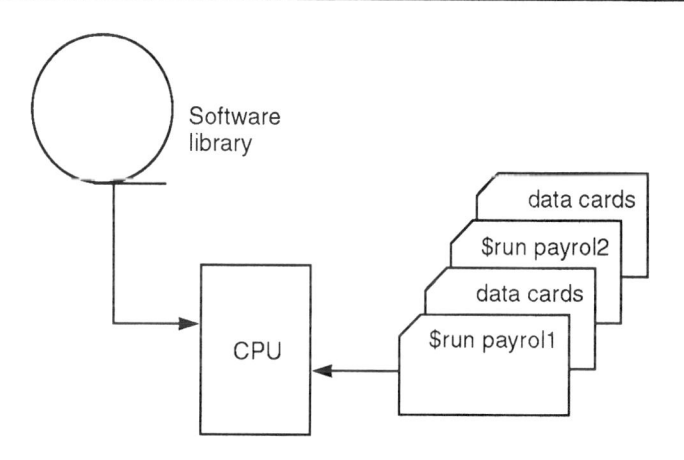

In second generation software environments, most automated software libraries were on reels of tape. By having computer commands imbedded within the data cards, the operators were able to plan their work schedules. (NOTE: In this example, I used the $ to identify job control statements. For several years, a variety of characters were used before the '//' became common.

Figure 2.3. Example of second-generation job control.

2.2.4. Need for multiprogramming as a cost control agent

The improvements up to this point helped the programmers and the operators, but they also revealed a major flaw in the environment: The computer was idle most of the time. Since most programs spend a majority of their elapsed time reading and writing to storage devices, the computer itself was usually doing nothing.

To get more work done, companies had to use several computers, and this added cost did not go unnoticed. There was a need for the computer operating software to do more than just schedule one job at a time. It also needed to optimize the idle time that was being wasted. If it could run more than one program at a time, this idle time could be put to productive use. This one feature, running more than one program at a time, opened up the future of mainframe computers as we see them today.

Multiprogramming is now common on the majority of mainframe computers (and several PCs) and was the turning point in making mainframe computers the major corporate resources that they are today. Making it happen required new hardware and new software because earlier computers were not designed for this function. IBM's System/360 computer would be a major part of the new generation.

SECTION REVIEW

The second generation was too short for me. It lacked structure, standards, common techniques, and even the languages were totally different from one computer model to another. The technical environment was usually simple enough for a person to actually master, a programmer's delight. The second generation was an important chapter, however, in the evolution of MVS. It set the stage for much of what we do today with mainframe computers.

CHAPTER REVIEW

My goal in this chapter was to review how computers operated before operating systems such as MVS arrived. I also wanted to share with you the productivity potential that MVS offered, productivity that is largely taken for granted today. If we look at how computers have improved over the last two decades, we see that large-scale, well-structured operating systems such as MVS are the foundation element. Faster hardware helped (and was required for MVS to be effective), but speed alone was not the key. An operating system that solved the problems of the earlier operating and programming environment was the solution everyone needed. MVS made it happen.

VOCABULARY REVIEW

These terms were introduced in this chapter. While not critical to your career success, knowing them will help you understand concepts and terminology in the information systems career field.

first generation

second generation

third generation

macro coding

IOCS

multiprogramming

program library

assembler language

The time: Wednesday morning, 9:00 A.M.

The location: A newly hired programmer's cubicle

"I sure hope I survive this first week at this company. At college, I was considered a computer guru, but I'm a know-nothing here. All the conversations about JCL, VSAM, IMS, TSO, ISPF, dump reading, hexadecimal arithmetic, and PROCLIBs are getting me down. I don't think I'll ever learn it all. Why didn't they teach us this at college? While at school, I felt that knowing COBOL was enough to get a secure future, and I thought that extra course on database theory and graphics design would be really relative here. Now, I find that the so-called "real world" wants more specific knowledge about software. MVS is a lot bigger than anything I ever imagined before.

"They talk a lot here about 24-hour availability, uploads, downloads, distributing data to remote sites, and software regression tests. I never knew there was so much to learn besides programming. It's exciting, but it's also scary. When I interviewed for the job, I should have asked about their training programs. Without some help, I don't know what to do first.

"I think an additional problem is that, at college, we all shared terminals in an open room and felt free to ask questions of each other. Here, it's just the opposite. Yes, this is an attractive cubicle they gave me, but the walls are so high I can't see anyone, and this dumb terminal just stares at me. If I could find my supervisor, maybe she would help me. Yeah, right.

"I wonder what this SYS REQ key is for... Uh-oh, what happened? Now the screen went blank! Now I've really messed things up, and it's just my first week."

3
History of MVS

MVS evolved from OS (Operating System), which was announced by IBM in 1964, along with the System/360 computer series. This was an exciting time for the computer community as, for the first time, IBM was offering a series of computers that had a high degree of compatibility from the smallest machine to the largest. Until then, most computers, even those from the same vendor, had different machine languages, different operating instructions, and different language compilers.

Looking back, some of the announced machines never made it into production. This was largely a case of offering more flexibility than was needed, but the industry had suffered for so long with incompatible equipment that the desire for a wide range of compatible machines is understandable. Also, some of the announced features were not available for several years. Still, the announcement of the System/360 and its associated support software (OS was one of many, but OS was the largest) was significant.

The durability of the basic design has been astonishing. While earlier computers had a lifespan of only a few years, a significant percentage of the System/360 product still lives on, almost 30 years after its announcement. (I recently had access to a 1969 version of the JCL manual. Interestingly, the majority of features — and the syntax — are still in current IBM

48 THE MVS PRIMER

documentation.) Clearly, an investment in learning the IBM OS environment was time well spent. Although systems programmers and other technical professionals will justifiably argue that the machine and the software have grown significantly in capability, the average programmer can still use 20-year-old reference material for many programming processes.

Everything you read here about OS also applies to MVS because MVS continued on with these facilities from OS, while adding more facilities to the list. I frequently read about the fast-changing computer field, yet a programmer trained in JCL, the Linkage Editor, and various OS utility programs, would be as productive today as in 1970. Many are.

3.1. S/360 ANNOUNCEMENT

The announcement of the System/360 computer was really an announcement of a family of computers. Each model shared the same instruction set, the same basic hardware components, and, to a degree, the same general operating software functions.

In reality, they were not fully compatible operationally. Migrating from a small machine to a much bigger one required a change in operating systems. Still, a user could easily upgrade from a smaller machine to a larger one and incur no conversion headaches if there were no change in the operating software. Since most computers in use at the time were small, this was not foreseen as a headache. (At the time, I recall my employer was planning to upgrade from a 16K IBM 1401 mainframe to a "big" IBM System/360 model 30 with 32K — a monster machine in 1966. The extra memory seemed a wasteful investment to me at the time.)

Because this isn't a hardware book (and I'm no hardware expert), let's look at what made the System/360 important from an evolutionary perspective. In a word, it was *interrupts*. Computers prior to the System/360 only obeyed instructions and were not designed to anticipate operating with more than one program. The System/360 was. Interrupts are the key to this flexibility. (Incidentally, the name of the System/360 was intended to show that it addressed the full circle — 360 degrees — of computing requirements.) Okay, so it was an innocent time, but the product forever changed how we view mainframes and computer economics. Now, let's discuss interrupts.

3.1.1. Hardware interrupts and their purpose

An *interrupt* is when the computer is interrupted from what it is doing and forced to execute a different set of code. This facility requires a close integration of the hardware and the software. For example, a divide instruction where the divisor is zero is mathematically impossible. On earlier machines, it may have caused an unpredictable quotient, or the computer may have just stopped. With the System/360, such an error caused the hardware to immediately interrupt the process. The built-in hardware analysis function diagnosed the cause of the problem and transferred control to a predefined (in the hardware) table of addresses.

To further complicate the process, the hardware needed to also automatically store sufficient information to allow the operating system to return control (optional) to the executing program or at least to provide adequate historical information to assist the programmer in debugging the cause of the interrupt — not an easy task.

This concept is not unlike the household with a family bulletin board. If all of the household members know to check the bulletin board for information, it becomes easy to notify others of changes in lifestyles, hobbies, jobs, and many other facets of life, because the notification process is structured. So it is with hardware interrupts. By designing the hardware to always give control to fixed hardware addresses, the designers of the operating system needed only to ensure that the address of the appropriate module was stored at the proper location within the table. See Figure 3.1 for a conceptual example.

While this may seem an artificial structure, the concept of allowing a machine to respond to interrupts is well founded in

50 THE MVS PRIMER

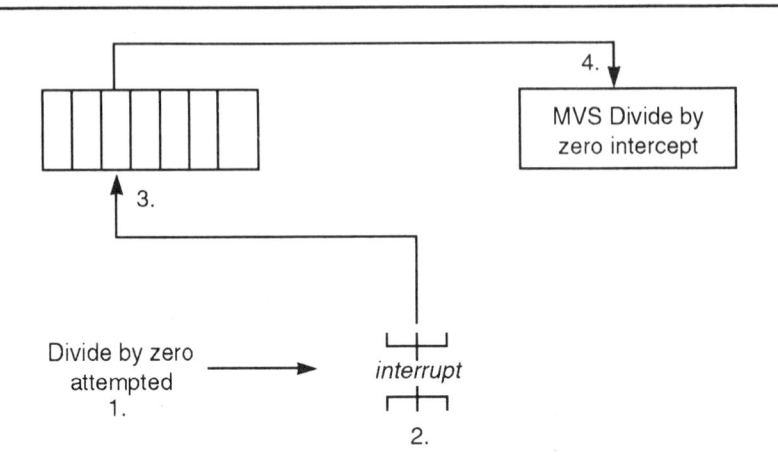

Step 1: Program commits an error.
Step 2: Hardware interrupt feature is activated.
Step 3: Hardware pulls address from predefined table.
Step 4: Appropriate MVS module receives control to process error.

Figure 3.1. Concept of hardware interrupt process.

all of our personal lives. For example, consider the following interrupts that all of us face:

- The telephone. This device is designed to alert us only when there is a call for us. (Consider how clumsy the device would be if we had to interrogate it for incoming calls.)

- The alarm clock or clock radio. Again, a device that is simple to operate and that lets us concentrate on other issues in our lives without worrying about time.

- The smoke alarm, the oven timer, the timer in the dryer, the door bell: All are examples of devices that are designed to interrupt us on demand but remain silent unless needed.

If you consider their impact on your life, all the devices just mentioned allow you the freedom to pursue a task, yet be able to respond immediately to another task, after which you can return to the original task — simple concept.

Clearly then, a computer with the ability to handle interrupts is a computer that has the potential to do several things. One of these things is to handle multiple programs concurrently — not simultaneously, but concurrently.

Consider the following conceptual example:

- Program X has caused a programming error (for example, a divide by zero). OS is interrupted to take charge of the situation.
- OS (now MVS) captures all the information about the problem and formats it for the programmer's use (called a *dump*).
- OS clears the program from the system and allows the next program in the queue to begin execution.
- OS gives control of the CPU to one of the other jobs that was executing concurrently with the failing program/job.

What happened here? Well, for one thing, the programmer gets information about the problem without needing to stop the computer (a step that was required in earlier computers). Also, the other programs that were in memory are unaware of the problem and continue to execute normally. This is critical to a data center, where there may be countless programs running at any one time. Having all of them terminated if any one of the programs has an error would be unacceptable today. This multiprogramming capability freed programmers from working a mandatory night shift to test new programs.

To repeat what was said earlier, interrupts are in the hardware, not in the software. Modern computers have preprogrammed capabilities today that are often beyond our imaginations. The capability to handle interrupts was one of the first that provided visible benefits. Some hardware interrupts were, however, accessible from application programs. Read on.

3.1.2. Fixed addresses for program services (SVCs)

The previous topic explained interrupts and how they would automatically intervene in certain situations. This concept of a predefined table of hardware addresses was also seen as beneficial to application programs.

Because IBM hardware and software designers worked together (an unusual project structure at the time), the software designers were able to request and obtain additional hardware features that aided the programming process. This facility was (and is) known as the Supervisor Call (SVC) instruction. The beauty of the SVC instruction was that it could be executed from within a program and possess all the benefits of predefined entries in the hardware interrupt table. The logic flow would be similar to that shown in Figure 3.1, as the hardware table of addresses is used for both situations.

Let's consider a typical example, a program needing to read a record. This gives an example of how the access method, which we have discussed, participates in a given program.

- The program executes an I/O instruction, such as OPEN, CLOSE, READ, or WRITE (in any IBM-supported language).

- The language compiler will have interpreted the command into the appropriate SVC instruction (each has a number following it).

- Upon execution, the appropriate address in the hardware table transfers control to the correct access method component to carry out the request.

This concept frees the compiler writers (or the programmer) from knowing the memory location of the proper OS/MVS routine. Again, this concept of providing a "directory" to MVS services made many other processes in the computer much simpler. In earlier years, such a concept may have seemed a waste of computer cycles. Today, it is seen as effective computer design.

3.1.3. I/O data channels

Now that you have a grasp of interrupts and SVCs, let's explore the concept of I/O channels. I/O channels were introduced in Chapter 1, where their basic intelligence was mentioned. Here we can review their true contribution to the S/360 environment.

In second-generation computers, the attachment of a device to the central processor was a single-process relationship. The S/360 system, however, isolated the central processor from the I/O devices, allowing them to be handled by specialized processors, known as I/O channels. When a read or write is issued in an application, the access method gives control to an I/O channel to do the required function. This frees the central processor from the I/O activity and also frees it from waiting for the I/O activity to occur. Both can be significant time-consuming activities (not unlike being placed on hold when you call someone — you're doing nothing but can't do anything.) A further benefit is that the operating system software need not be upgraded each time there is a hardware modification.

With this structure, an S/360 system could be doing several processes, not just concurrently, but simultaneously; one program could be executing, and each I/O channel could be coordinating an I/O request. This one improvement increased the system's capability to handle large workloads, a task that would guarantee MVS's future position in corporate business.

3.1.4. Instruction set and registers

Second-generation computers typically had instruction sets that related to the physical reality of a "one-program" machine. In other words, because a computer could run only one program, the programmer was able to decide which memory addresses would be used. If this would be the only program in memory, location was not a concern.

The S/360 changed that way of thinking. Since there could be several programs in memory, the programs needed to be designed so they could be relocated to different memory locations for each execution with no loss of function. That meant that instructions needed to be written so that their true computer address could be resolved at the time of execution. IBM solved this issue by using a register-displacement concept. For example, instead of referencing an instruction or a data area by a specific memory address, the S/360 compilers generated code to reference memory as a register value plus a displacement offset. The compilers also generated code to place the appropriate values into registers at the time execution began. (Note: A *register* is a fixed address in the computer with a fixed size. In the IBM MVS series of computers, there are 16 registers, each with a size of 32 bits.) Let's look at an example:

> A program is written to use register 4 to contain the beginning address for a data area and use offset values to reflect a data area. Let's use COBOL to simplify a small example:
>
> 01   DATA-AREA.
>
>   05   FIRST-FIELD   PIC   X(8).
>
>   05   SECOND-FIELD   PIC   X(5).
>
>   05   THIRD-FIELD   PIC   X(5).

If register 4 were used by the COBOL compiler to contain the address of DATA-AREA, the data item called THIRD-FIELD would be addressed by using the contents of register 4, plus a displacement of 13 (the number of bytes beyond that address).

An instruction such as:

MOVE SECOND-FIELD TO THIRD-FIELD

would generate machine code that represented the following:

> Move the five bytes, beginning at the eighth byte plus the value of register 4, to the thirteenth byte plus the value of register 4.

The advantage of this technique is that the instruction will work correctly, no matter where the data area is, assuming that register 4 has been preloaded with the correct value. Unfortunately, the maximum offset that can be used is 4,096, requiring that the 16 registers be frequently stored with new values. If you were to do a detailed review of machine instructions from any MVS language compiler, you would find that many of the instructions were just managing the contents of the registers, not doing the application logic. Obviously, this is a juggling act but an important and necessary one. In earlier computers, the memory address was fixed, since there was only one program executing. Consider the comparison in Figure 3.2.

Sample instructions to add one data field to another:

Second generation: A   425   896

(Add the field in memory location 425 to the field in memory location 896)

System/360:   AP   5   896   6   425   3

(Add a 5-byte field, located at 425 bytes + register 3 to the field located at 896 bytes + register 6)

Figure 3.2. Second- versus third-generation instructions.

Note: In the preceding paragraph, a computer limit was mentioned — a maximum offset of 4,096. As you study computers, you need to be aware that such limits are not arbitrary (for example, why not have a limit of 5,000, or maybe no limit at all?). In this particular case, there is a maximum offset limit of 4,096 because only 12 bits in a System/360 or System/370 series computer are allocated for the offset value. That was a design decision. If you are familiar with binary numbers, you know that there are 4,096 different values in 12 bits (0 through 4,095). An awareness of binary maximums will always help you understand why a particular limit exists within any computer.

SECTION REVIEW

My intent in this section was not for you to master computer hardware but for you to grasp some of the concepts of how it all works. There is no magic in MVS, and I hope this section was helpful to you. If you program in an MVS environment, you may find that this basic information is too frequently omitted from training or reference material.

3.2.   OS COMPONENTS

While I will never know all the components of MVS or of OS, it is important that you know that MVS and OS were not single software programs, but they represent hundreds of separate programs and products that, together, form what we call an operating system. If you ever work at more than one MVS data center, you will find that some features that were at the former data center aren't at (or work somewhat differently from) the present one, and you will also find some components at the new data center that weren't at the previous one. This ability to customize the operating system to meet a company's requirements is an important factor, considering the enormous investment that an MVS corporate data center represents.

3.2.1. OS/360 — the basics

By now, you can visualize the major components of OS (called OS/360). It came fully packaged, including support for JCL, a linkage editor, access methods, an assembler language, many data utility programs, and several high-level programming languages (e.g., COBOL, FORTRAN, PL/1). This was indeed an operating system that omitted nothing for its time. An installation with OS had no need to order additional software from IBM. It was all there.

As the software industry matured, this would change. Utility software products, compilers, and system management software products would eventually compete with IBM's offerings, but the customer benefitted from this. With competition, the quality of software improved, and more options became available. It is a rare installation today that does not have several non-IBM products among its most important software components. On the plus side, all major components are much improved today; on the minus side, MVS today has fewer major components built in to its basic structure. No longer may a company only consider the cost of hardware. Software is now a major consideration in all budgets for information systems departments.

Operationally, OS brought about a major change in how a computer room was staffed and operated. In the second generation, programmers were often free to operate the computer —

and frequently did it better because they were familiar with the peculiarities of their programs. With OS, the job of operating a large computer became a major career field. Since the computer could run many jobs concurrently, the operators needed to do complex scheduling to keep the system working to its capacity. To do less would require that the company invest in more computers to do the work. Instead of playing solo, the operator was now a conductor.

This change put increased demands on the computer operations staff (by now its own department), including the need to develop new skills. OS, being a constantly resident program, transformed the perception of a computer from just a piece of equipment to a living creature. Using a console typewriter, operators entered a complex language of mnemonics and hieroglyphic symbols to communicate instructions (and replies to OS's requests). In most shops, programmers were no longer welcome in the computer room, and they would soon be banned completely. (Note: Although I have had many important jobs and titles in my 26+ years in the computer field, I haven't been in a computer room more than twice in the past 15 years — and both of those trips were with an assigned escort from whose side I could not stray.)

One of the major tasks for operators was handling an IPL (Initial Program Load). The System/360 computer could not be started just by turning on a power switch. Since the hardware and software were developed to work together, no application programs could run until OS was started; not an easy task. While powerful, OS was still a giant of a program (and MVS is much, much bigger still) that needed to be coaxed and prodded into full awareness and control. This was done through the initial program load. When an operator pressed the load button, the hardware would attempt to find the first few instructions of OS, which had (supposedly) been placed on a specific track on a specific disk drive. If the initial instructions were found, the IPL would continue; if not, systems programmers would be called to locate and fix the problem. Assuming the initial instructions were found, the start-up process (some would

58 THE MVS PRIMER

call it a fire drill because the process often took an unexpected turn) went something like this.

- The initial instructions would locate the next higher level of program code and give control to it. The only need for the IPL code was to get the process moving.

- The next higher level of code would do an elementary check of the computer environment (amount of memory, number of tape drives, number and location of disk drives), reporting any errors to the operator and demanding (not asking) that unresolved device addresses be reconciled. This might require scurrying around the computer room to determine what devices were not powered up or had been moved (physically or electrically).

- With the physical configuration accounted for, OS would prompt for instructions on what classes of jobs to run, how much memory to allocate to each, and other issues that would assist it in doing the day's workload. It took a skilled operator to ensure that correct responses were given to all the prompts. If errors occurred, it was often necessary to start all over again.

- The entire process (more complex than I demonstrated here) requires approximately 20 to 30 minutes and must be done each time the computer is restarted. In the early days of OS, there were lots of program bugs, so this was sometimes done several times a day. In today's world of MVS, the IPL process is rarely needed but is still capable of getting my adrenalin flowing because it is a complex and critical event.

3.2.2. System administration — utilities

In the previous topic I mentioned some data utilities. While these are still supplied by IBM, many of their functions are more easily obtained by using non-IBM software. In fact, most programmers today are not even trained in how to use them. Still, since they are included in the basic software package, they have untapped value. Several are commonly used; several are never used. Here are names of some of the more commonly used ones.

IEBGENER (pronounced *eye-bee-gin-er* or just *gin-er*): This program copies one file to another and is frequently used by programmers for this simple task.

IEBCOPY (pronounced *eye-bee-copy*): Rarely used in many installations, this is helpful for managing partitioned data sets (explained in next topic). With the popularity today of ISPF, this utility is used less than in earlier years.

IEBPTPCH (pronounced *eye-bee-print-punch*): This utility was helpful to print files, but it is used less today because users have the ability to browse files from computer terminals via ISPF or other software products.

3.2.3. Programming facilities and libraries

OS provided several services to programmers that are still in use today, largely due to the sound design of these services. You may recall from Chapter 2 that there was little structure to the programming process and few tools to help. OS standardized the entire process, thereby ensuring that programs written for this environment would not suffer from the filing cabinet approach to organizing and structuring programs that was common prior to the System/360 and OS. With OS, a programmer could write a program in one language and also use the services of a program written in another language. Also, once compiled into executable code, the executable code could be made part of other programs. Let's see how this was accomplished.

OS allowed executable programs (the MVS term for an executable program is *load module*) to be created by only *one* program. This program is called the Linkage Editor because it has the capability to link different programs together into one executable unit. The Linkage Editor is to MVS what cement is to a building foundation. Whether a program is written in COBOL, FORTRAN, PL/1, or some other language, it must be converted by the Linkage Editor before it can be executed. This single path to program development ensures that certain controls can be in place and also provides a common language for programmers to share, regardless of the programming language they use.

Access to the Linkage Editor is usually easy and provides a high degree of control in itself. Without access to the Linkage Editor, programmers would face mountains of red tape to get anything accomplished. Unfortunately, while JCL and the Linkage Editor are the two major foundation elements of MVS, neither of the subjects is routinely taught to new programmers. Often, this happens because new programmers are given copies of sample JCL and Linkage Editor instructions that work. Since this gets the task accomplished, there is little incentive for programmers to investigate the relationship. See Figure 3.3 for an example of the programming process for OS (and MVS).

The load modules created by the Linkage Editor are stored in special datasets called *libraries*. Terms commonly used for such

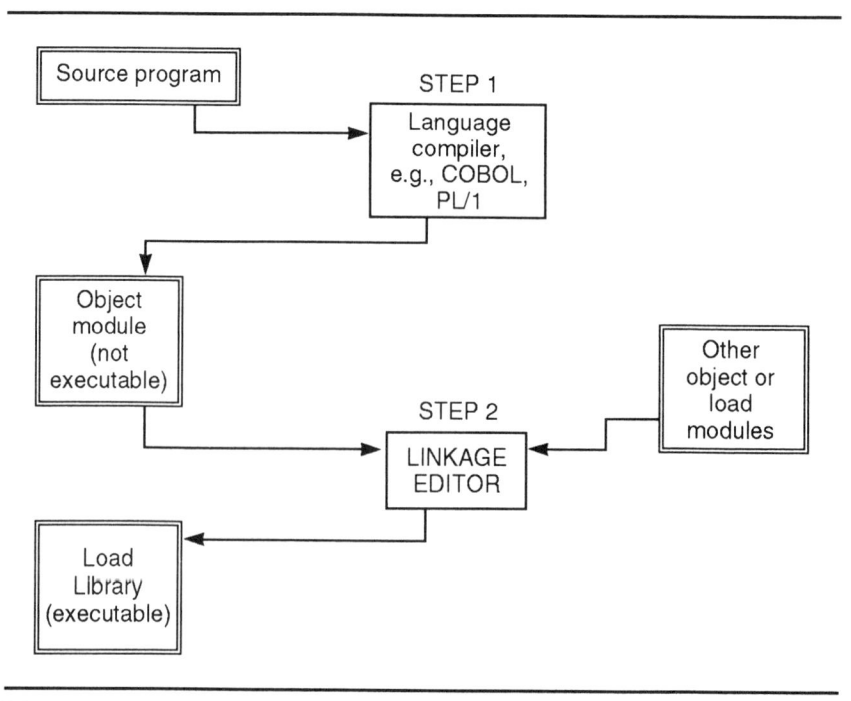

Figure 3.3. Example of the two-step compile/link process.

libraries that contain load modules are LINKLIB and PGMLIB (pronounced *pig-um-libe*). (Reminder: You will never be considered to be MVS-literate unless you pronounce abbreviations properly, even those with no vowels.) The analogy to a brick-and-mortar library is excellent. An MVS library is a dataset that can contain many individual entries (called *members*), much as a public library contains many books. Usually a library dataset contains either load modules or JCL statements. Because a library dataset is partitioned into many smaller *datasets*, it is referred to as a partitioned dataset (PDS). By grouping many programs into a single library dataset, an installation or department exerts significant control in maintaining an inventory of authorized programs. To provide quick access to each member in the library, a PDS dataset will always contain a directory that identifies the track location for the beginning of each member (similar to the VTOC you read about previously). See Figure 3.4 for an example of a PDS.

I mentioned in Chapter 1 that MVS had a separate search route to locate programs. First, make sure you're comfortable with the search path for data, shown in Figure 1.7. There you saw that a JCL statement identified the need for MVS to locate it. That particular JCL statement is called a *DD* statement because it is used to *define data*. (If you check Figure 1.7, you will see that DD appears on the statement.)

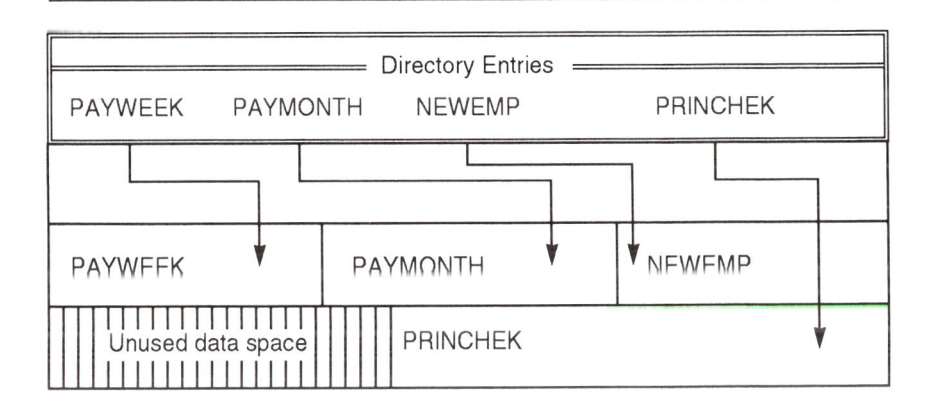

Figure 3.4. Example of PDS concepts.

Now, let's review how MVS locates programs. When we first saw Figure 1.2, I said that I would explain statement 2 in Figure 1.2 later. Statement 2 (the word *JOBLIB* appears on it) can be used to tell MVS the name of the PDS library that MVS should search to find the load modules for the particular job. The programs themselves are identified on JCL statements that contain the word *EXEC* (statement 3 in Figure 1.2 is an example).

An additional approach provided by MVS is through a list of authorized libraries established by the installation's systems programmers. This feature (often called the *linklist*) allows programmers and other users to execute programs without knowing in which library the programs reside. This simplifies use of the computer and provides significant controls to a company. Programs that will be used by a wide audience of users are usually stored in a library that is identified in the linklist. When this is done, the JCL statement identified in the previous paragraph (JOBLIB) is not needed.

Like the libraries for load modules, JCL libraries are also partitioned. Unlike the libraries for load modules, JCL libraries for system functions are allocated only by systems programmers to ensure that unauthorized JCL isn't submitted to MVS. By now you recognize the importance and power of JCL. Allowing certain system-oriented JCL to be provided by unauthorized users could create havoc within the system environment. JCL libraries are referred to as PROCLIBs because JCL subsets are called PROCs (for PROCedures).

Programmers may write JCL procedures, but systems programmers play the librarian's role of properly identifying and cataloging the separate members.

SECTION REVIEW

This section covered basic material that, to this day, is still a part of MVS. The terms used here (PROCLIBs, load modules, JCL, utilities, partitioned data sets, IEBGENER) are common terms, and some familiarity with them will help you master more complex concepts as your experience in MVS expands.

3.3. OS TO MVS EVOLUTION

Obviously, neither OS nor MVS had their eventual capacity at their first availability. They evolved from what had gone before. While the evolution is too complex for this book (and any attempt — including the one I make here — will alienate more knowledgeable readers), here is a quick overview of the parentage of MVS (see Figure 3.5).

First there was OS. It came in two major forms, MFT (multi programming for a fixed number of tasks) and MVT (multi programming for a variable number of tasks). (Note: There was also a third version, PCP (Primary Control Program), but since it only controlled one task, it had a short life.) In general, midrange computers (up to a whopping 256K or so of memory) used MFT. Those with more memory (512K) and more add-on components —

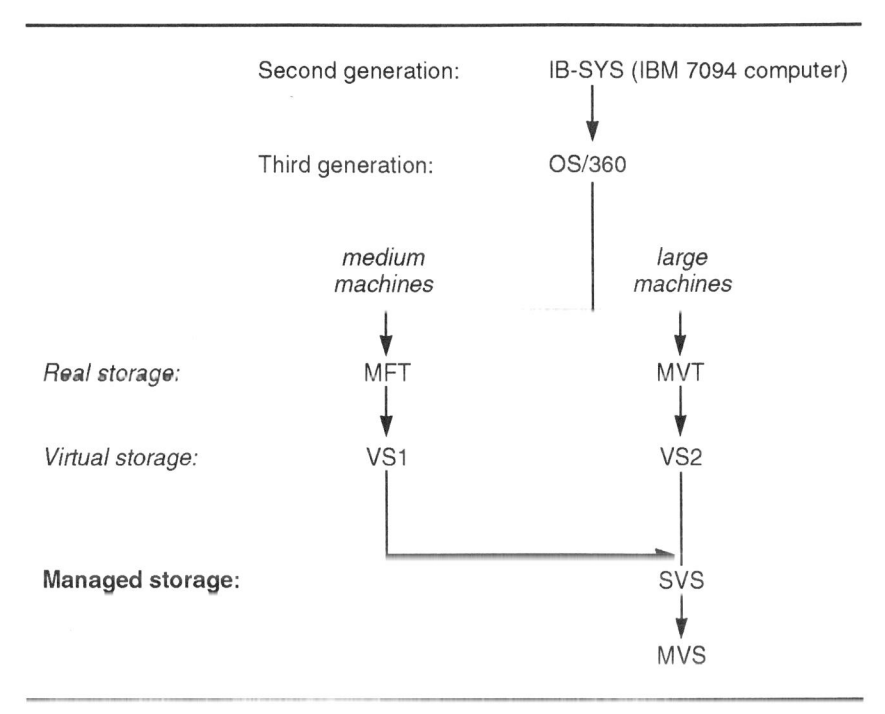

	Second generation:	IB-SYS (IBM 7094 computer)
		↓
	Third generation:	OS/360
	medium machines	*large machines*
	↓	↓
Real storage:	MFT	MVT
	↓	↓
Virtual storage:	VS1	VS2
		↓
Managed storage:		SVS
		↓
		MVS

Figure 3.5. Evolution of OS to MVS.

the biggest data centers — used MVT. MFT required approximately 120K of memory, not dissimilar to the requirements for a PC-based operating system today. MVT, on the other hand, could chew up much larger bites of memory for its services. (Yes, it was possible — if the systems programmers weren't careful — for MVT to use more memory than the applications did.)

While MFT handled most needs for the day, MVT held the promise of the future. Getting customers to use it would require making memory cheaper and more available. The concept of virtual memory made that happen.

As virtual memory management became available (explained in next topic), it was offered to both MFT and MVT users as VS1 and VS2, respectively. These products provided the same services as their predecessors but removed the constraint of memory availability.

As applications became more sophisticated, each version evolved into a 16-megabyte version, called SVS (single virtual storage) and MVS (multiple virtual storage). Where SVS provided 16 megabytes to all users to share (I thought that was more than enough for all eternity at the time), MVS provided 16 megabytes to *each* application. Today, even this is considered insufficient for major corporate mission-critical applications. In time, SVS users migrated to MVS, leaving it as the successor to a long line of interesting products. (Note: The amount of memory allocated to a job, such as the 16 megabytes that MVS allocated to each job, is known as an *address space*.).

OS/360 served a useful life and through it all maintained a common interface to programmers and applications, preventing any requirement for major application conversions or for retraining. (In the first and second generations, any change usually required that all programs be completely rewritten and tested, obviously not an economical undertaking for a company.) MVS is now the primary IBM operating system for large mainframes, providing an image of all virtual storage (address space) to each job in the system. A conceptual comparison of sharing a single image of virtual storage versus having one for each job is shown in Figure 3.6.

HISTORY OF MVS   65

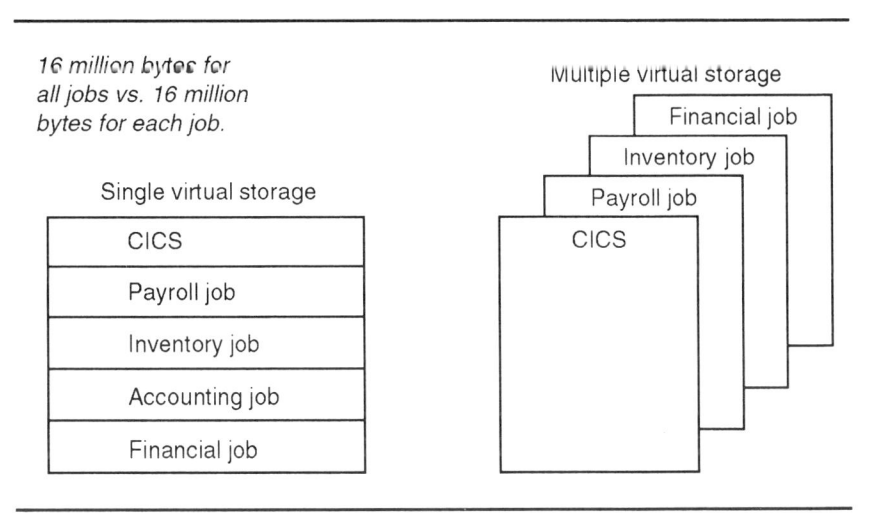

```
16 million bytes for                    Multiple virtual storage
all jobs vs. 16 million              ┌─────────────────┐
bytes for each job.                  │  Financial job  │
                                  ┌──┴──────────────┐  │
                                  │  Inventory job  │  │
   Single virtual storage      ┌──┴──────────────┐  │──┘
  ┌─────────────────────┐      │  Payroll job    │  │
  │        CICS         │      │                 │──┘
  ├─────────────────────┤      │      CICS       │
  │    Payroll job      │      │                 │
  ├─────────────────────┤      │                 │
  │    Inventory job    │      │                 │
  ├─────────────────────┤      │                 │
  │    Accounting job   │      │                 │
  ├─────────────────────┤      │                 │
  │    Financial job    │      │                 │
  └─────────────────────┘      └─────────────────┘
```

Figure 3.6. Comparison of SVS and MVS.

3.3.1.   Memory management

Earlier I reviewed task management, whereby MVS allows several jobs to share the CPU and other resources. One of the resources that all jobs share is memory. Whenever MVS authorizes a new job to start, an initial allocation of memory is made for the job. This allocation is called a *region*. (If you refer back to Figure 1.9, there are four regions because there are four jobs.) The amount of memory allocated is either a predefined default for the data center (established by the systems programmers) or an amount specified by the job's JCL.

Memory is allocated in thousand-byte units (called *kilobytes* and usually shortened to K). Five thousand bytes would usually be written as 5K. In truth, however, one K is not one thousand bytes (1000) but one thousand twenty-four bytes (1024), because the system uses a binary numbering system and there is no multiple of 2 that equals 1000. The difference is only 24 bytes, but the variance of 24 becomes significant as you start to reach larger numbers. Consider a mainframe with millions of bytes of memory. A megabyte (one million bytes) is really 1,048,576 bytes, creating a difference of over 48,500 for each megabyte. If you're wondering, "Why the dissertation on numbering systems?", it is because I want you to be aware that the JCL that requests 100,000 bytes of memory does not get the same amount of memory as the JCL that requests 100K of memory.

Once upon a time all memory was *real*. By real I mean that you could open the computer cover and reach in and touch it. If a company wanted more memory, it had to buy it or (as was usually the case) buy a larger computer. Programmers could still develop programs that were too large to fit into memory, but that required a complex (and costly) programming process that developed programs into *overlays*, a rarely used technique due to cost and complexity. For these reasons, memory was a tightly controlled resource. A typical programming specification was how much memory the final program could use, regardless of the processing requirement. Not anymore. MVS uses *virtual memory* for most memory assignments, freeing applications from the restriction on memory use, and programmers from even knowing how much memory is required. There is an example of virtual memory in Figure 3.7.

Although it may sound complicated, the concept of virtual memory couldn't be simpler. For example, you probably work at a virtual desk. What does that mean? It means that, even though you may work on many projects, the paperwork for all of them will fit on your desktop. So, your desktop has no virtual limit. (Obviously, you would need a desk much larger if all the paperwork of your job had to fit on the desktop *at the same time*, but that wasn't part of my definition, was it?) All of your paperwork fits on your desk because you periodically move paperwork that isn't needed into drawers and file cabinets and also move needed paperwork from drawers and file cabinets onto your desk top. That simple process, storing what isn't immediately needed *to* a storage device and recalling what is needed *from* a storage device is all there is to the concept of virtual memory.

Virtual memory came into widespread use with the Burroughs B-5500 mainframe computer in the mid-1960s. Until that time, whenever a program was loaded into memory, the entire program had to be there, even though only a portion of the program was in use. The Burroughs machine created executable programs that

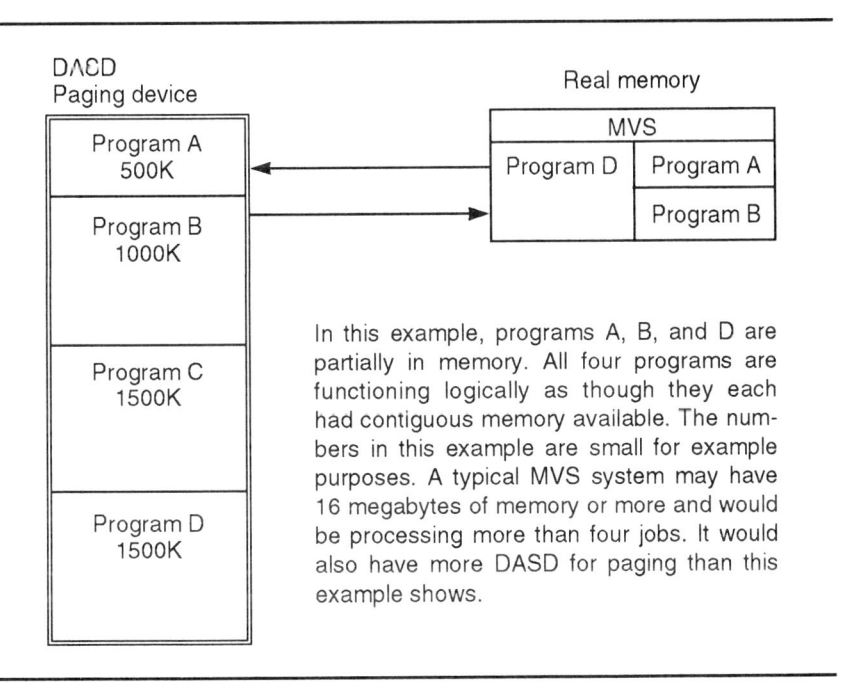

```
DASD                                  Real memory
Paging device                    ┌──────────────────────┐
┌─────────────────┐              │         MVS          │
│    Program A    │◄─────────────┤ Program D │Program A │
│      500K       │              ├───────────┴──────────┤
├─────────────────┤─────────────►│      Program B       │
│    Program B    │              └──────────────────────┘
│     1000K       │
│                 │        In this example, programs A, B, and D are
├─────────────────┤        partially in memory. All four programs are
│    Program C    │        functioning logically as though they each
│     1500K       │        had contiguous memory available. The num-
│                 │        bers in this example are small for example
│                 │        purposes. A typical MVS system may have
├─────────────────┤        16 megabytes of memory or more and would
│    Program D    │        be processing more than four jobs. It would
│     1500K       │        also have more DASD for paging than this
│                 │        example shows.
└─────────────────┘
```

Figure 3.7. Example of virtual storage.

were made up of segments (sometimes called *pages*) that allowed the operating system to keep in memory only those segments that were immediately required. The segments not being used were written to DASD and brought into memory as needed. By moving pieces of programs to and from memory, the illusion was created that there was virtually no limit to the computer's memory. The mechanics of moving memory images to and from memory is known as *paging*. When the workload is well balanced, the extra overhead needed for the operating system to perform this feat is usually not noticed. When the system has too many programs competing for the real memory, the act of paging consumes more CPU resources than the applications do. This overload situation is known as *thrashing*. A system that frequently encounters thrashing needs more memory (so that more memory is available to the competing applications), fewer running programs (so there is less competition for available memory), or faster DASD (so the delay in processing is less significant).

68 THE MVS PRIMER

Despite the success of the B-5500, virtual memory did not become a popular term until it was widely used to describe the RCA Spectra series of computers in the late 1960s and the early 1970s. Within a few years, virtual memory was the major way to manage memory on major mainframe systems.

The management of memory, indeed its allocation, is a complex marriage between hardware and software. For example, while a program may think it is executing a program instruction at a particular address that doesn't physically exist, the hardware can only execute instructions in real memory. Doing this successfully requires that MVS juggle both the virtual and the physical addresses. For now, just assume that any job can access several million bytes of memory, regardless of the real memory available.

3.3.2. Emergence of MVS job scheduling facilities

When OS was announced, job input and output scheduling was accomplished by two different products that followed the format of other job processes. They worked, but they were clumsy. These two OS components were known as *readers* and *writers*.

A reader was an OS component that would read JCL from a given device into the scheduling function. The process of reading jobs competed with the process of executing jobs. (For example, it was not uncommon for an OS computer to be unable to schedule new work until current work was completed.)

Likewise, writers were OS components that also competed with executing jobs. The writers were tasks that printed the various reports that had been prepared by a previously executed job.

To execute a single job or a series of jobs, the operator needed to tell OS (via the console typewriter) to

1. start a reader to read in the job;
2. tell the initiator to run the job; and
3. start a writer to print the output.

These steps were clumsy and interfered with the task of getting the jobs done. A superior solution came from a user-written set of programs called HASP (Houston Automatic Spooling Priority system). The HASP programs were free to IBM customers and eliminated the need for the readers and writers, plus they added major enhancements to the function of scheduling work into the computer. An additional benefit of HASP was its ability to communicate with remote computers, allowing any remote site to operate as if it was scheduling its own mainframe computer. Where OS/360 scheduled tasks of currently executing jobs, HASP scheduled the jobs into the system and the output from the system. See Figure 3.8.

IBM quickly recognized the value of HASP and integrated many of its processes (and even its code) into a fully supported set of IBM software known as Job Entry Subsystem 2 (JES2, pronounced *jez two*). (Note: Most MVS shops today use JES2 for scheduling work and distributing printed output. While you will see the JES acronym, you will also continue to see HASP on many messages. My grapevine tells me that HASP was developed by NASA at Houston, but I can't confirm that. If readers will write and tell me about it, I'd be glad to include the information in the next edition of this book.)

While HASP was providing new direction to the job scheduling function, a different product, ASP (Attached System Processor), was developed to link multiple mainframes together,

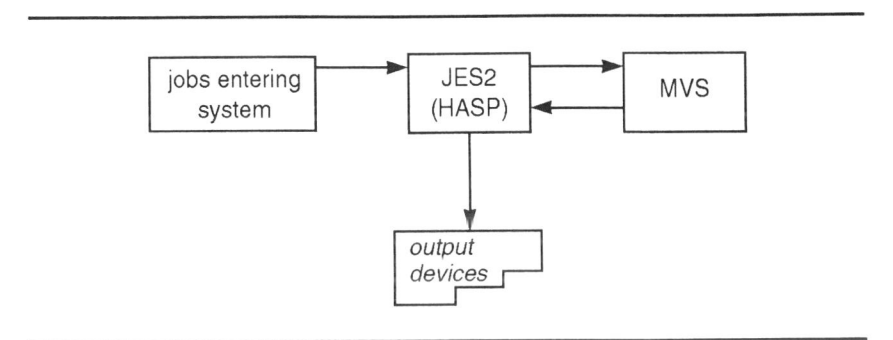

Figure 3.8. Example of JES2 job flow.

presenting the perception of a single computer when, in fact, there might be several of them. ASP was instrumental in the development of a global computer, allowing operators and users to *see* one computer, yet have the benefits of backup and the power of several computers. ASP became Job Entry Subsystem 3 (JES3). I admit to never working with JES3, so I have no experiences to share. Still, JES3 is a fascinating system. If your company is using JES3, it is probably a large corporation or one with a significant need to be continuously available.

ASP (now JES3) achieved its result by having a master/slave relationship among the many processors. One was the global processor, and it directed work to the other processors. If any of the computers required maintenance, its work could be redirected. Likewise, if the global processor needed maintenance, another processor could be instructed to assume its role. See Figure 3.9 for an example.

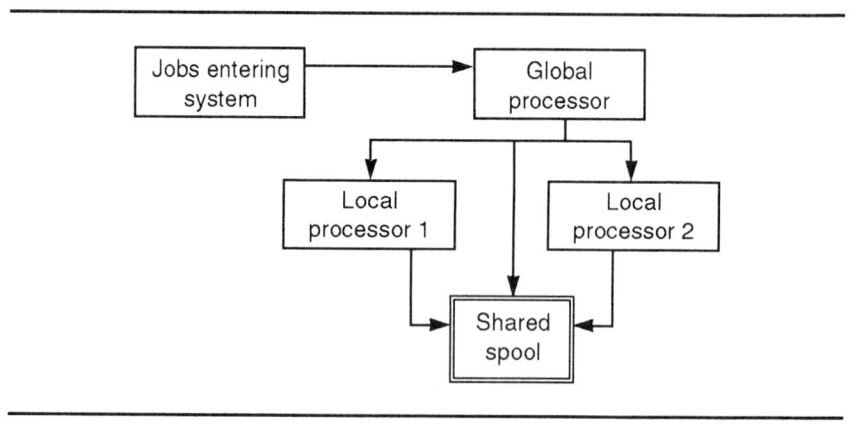

Figure 3.9. Example of JES3 facilities.

In Figure 3.9 there are three mainframes, all sharing in a common pool of work. The shared spool DASD device keeps them in touch with each other. This concept can be extended to remote facilities. For more information on JES3, see the suggested reading material in Chapter 7.

3.3.3. Emergence of online and database facilities

The original OS/360 was all batch. There were no significant online facilities. After all, batch was all that was needed in the mid-1960s. That situation didn't last long as, within a few years, online features were not only desired but necessary. By the early 1970s, many companies needed access to their systems from desktop terminals.

At the time, the term database had little meaning. IBM provided an indexed access method (called ISAM and pronounced *eye-sam*) that allowed companies to develop direct-access files, but a database (the linking of related data into its own structure) was not available. As the need for online systems grew, the need for ways to organize data became important. The following software additions are mentioned briefly here but are more fully explained in the next chapter.

The first to come was TSO, because it supported the programming community (the use of computer terminals by user personnel was still in the future). TSO expanded OS/360 by allowing programmers access to computing facilities without having to allow the programmers into the computer room.

IMS came next, providing a facility to organize data in the way companies used it. Some online facilities were available, and there were backup and restart features that were not available elsewhere.

CICS began life on midsized mainframes and was just for transaction management. For a time, it seemed to have a limited lifespan, but it has been expanded over time to have many of the features of IMS while retaining a significant amount of flexibility.

SECTION REVIEW

This section presented the MVS fundamentals that you will often see today. Virtual memory, JES, transaction managers such as IMS/DC and/or CICS, and TSO are facts of life in most MVS installations. The next chapter will give you more in-depth awareness of some of these products.

CHAPTER REVIEW

This chapter presented the foundation elements that allowed OS to evolve into MVS as we see it today. Virtual storage, job scheduling facilities, online access, and database systems were all key components of MVS's emergence into a major operating environment.

VOCABULARY REVIEW

Okay, so it was a big chapter. That gives you more words to learn, right? You should probably reread this chapter and then review some of the new words, many of which are listed here.

interrupt

PROCLIB

reader

writer

JES2

JES3

TSO

virtual memory

IMS

CICS

I/O channels

MFT and MVT

The time: Wednesday afternoon, 1.00 P.M.

The location: The help desk

"Wow. 'Hump day' is here. The week is half over, and I'm over the hump. Friday night can't come soon enough for me. The phone here seems to ring nonstop, and I sure need the break on the weekend. I get calls from people because they forgot their password, can't turn their terminal on, can't find their reports, or just because they're confused. I even had a programmer call the other day when he pressed the SYS REQ key. That sure can destroy a terminal session. I tried to reassure him that it was no big deal. Fixing the problem just took me a few seconds. He sure sounded frightened.

"Actually, I love this job. Talking with everyone from vice-presidents to programmers to clerical personnel makes me feel good, because I get the chance to solve a problem for each of them. Most of the calls are from people who appreciate my help. I get lots of 'Gee, thanks' from them. One fellow even brought me a couple of doughnuts. The tough part of the job is handling the 1 percent of employees who seem to feel that it's my fault that they have a problem. Just yesterday, a manager tried to sign on from one terminal while he was still signed on at another terminal. That's not my problem that RACF refused to allow it. That's security, man. No one person can be signed on to the computer from more than one terminal. Boy, did I hear lots of swear words. I don't think he realizes that several thousand people are logged onto this system and that security is important to all of us.

"Once, I worked the night shift on help desk. Boy, that was interesting. I talked with programmers working at home, out-of-state office managers getting data into the system, and I even got to talk to the office manager in our Berlin office. I had always thought nothing happened in the data center after 5:00 P.M. I learned a lot about 24-hour data centers that night."

4

Online Access and Databases

As the previous chapter showed, the needs for both access to the computer and organization of data to particular needs grew rapidly. The products known as TSO, IMS, CICS, and DB2 emerged to meet these growing demands. Today, they are routinely considered as part of the growing world of MVS.

4.1. TSO

TSO (for Time Sharing Option) was one of the first online components of OS/360, and it was optional (it required more memory). TSO (always spelled out; never pronounced) was the gate opener to improving programmer productivity because it allowed programmers to do program development from typewriter terminals instead of through punched cards. Being able to correct errors and resubmit jobs without an intervening keypunch operator or job scheduling clerk allowed programmers to get more than one job run per day (quite a feat in the early 1970s).

By the late 1970s, TSO supported video display terminals (VDTs, also known as cathode ray terminals or CRTs), and a full-screen product, ISPF (Interactive Structured Programming Facility) became available. ISPF not only relieved the programmer from using commands that were designed for typewriter terminals, it also presented an easily modifiable menu from which an exhaustive list of utility and edit functions were available. This became the foundation at many companies for their *programmer tool box*. Today, most MVS systems use TSO and ISPF to support the programming process.

SECTION REVIEW

For programmers, TSO is often the most visible aspect of MVS. It is available nowhere else and provides an extensive array of programming tools, especially if combined with ISPF. I use TSO and ISPF daily and would be incapable of doing my work without them. A programmer or analyst without TSO and ISPF is like a truck driver without a truck.

4.2. IMS AND DL/I

Whereas TSO was an online tool developed by IBM to improve programmer productivity, DL/I (Data/Language I) was developed to allow companies to use IBM's existing access methods but with an intervening program that managed the data so it retained a predefined structure. DL/I is considered a programming language but not in the same sense as COBOL. Instead, DL/I is a set of procedural codes and values that are used to communicate with the intervening program, called IMS (for Information Management System). To use DL/I, a programmer must first know a programming language such as COBOL, PL/1, or Assembler. The programmer uses the programming language to send DL/I requests to IMS (interestingly, always spelled; never pronounced) which, in turn, processes the request. The use of DL/I is evidenced by the appearance of certain statements within a program. Here is a COBOL example:

```
    MOVE EMPLOYEE-ID TO FILE-READ-KEY
    CALL 'CBLTDLI' USING GU
          EMPLOYEE-PCB
          EMPLOYEE-SEGMENT
          EMPLOYEE-SSA
    IF PCB-STATUS-CODE = SPACE
       MOVE EMPLOYEE-NAME TO PRINT-RECORD
```

As the above example shows, the DL/I language consists of data fields that are passed to the IMS Interface program using the traditional CALL statement. The status code field must always be checked to ensure that the DL/I request was a valid one. Because the data fields control what is to happen, DL/I coding errors cannot be trapped by the language compiler but must be found during actual execution. For this reason, IBM offers a separate software product to assist in program testing. It is called BTS (Batch and Terminal Simulator).

IMS data structures are considered to be hierarchical, i.e., data is viewed as an inverted tree (branches are at the bottom, not at the top). Many people prefer this structure as it is easily understood. For example, a manufacturing company might want to organize a database of its assembly parts to include information about suppliers and about the inventory in various warehouses. Such a data hierarchy might look like the one in Figure 4.1.

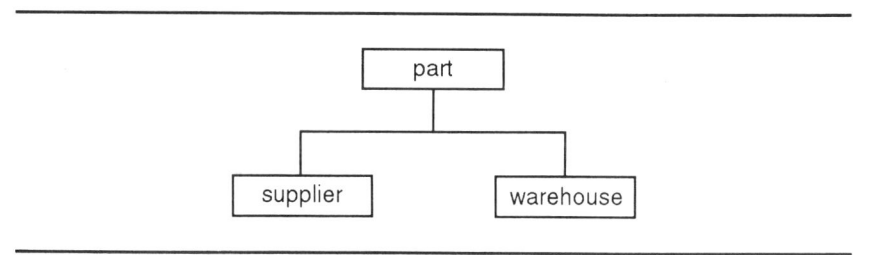

```
         ┌──────┐
         │ part │
         └──┬───┘
      ┌─────┴─────┐
┌──────────┐  ┌───────────┐
│ supplier │  │ warehouse │
└──────────┘  └───────────┘
```

Figure 4.1. Example of IMS database structure.

Each "box" in Figure 4.1 is called a segment and contains data fields specific to its purpose. For example, the *part* segment might contain part number, retail price, description. The *supplier* segment might contain supplier name, address, and phone number. The *warehouse* segment might contain items in inventory for this part number and an identifying warehouse code. The power of the IMS structure becomes more apparent when you see that each segment may occur indefinitely. While the previous example was of a theoretical database structure, see Figure 4.2 for an example of a real database record using that structure.

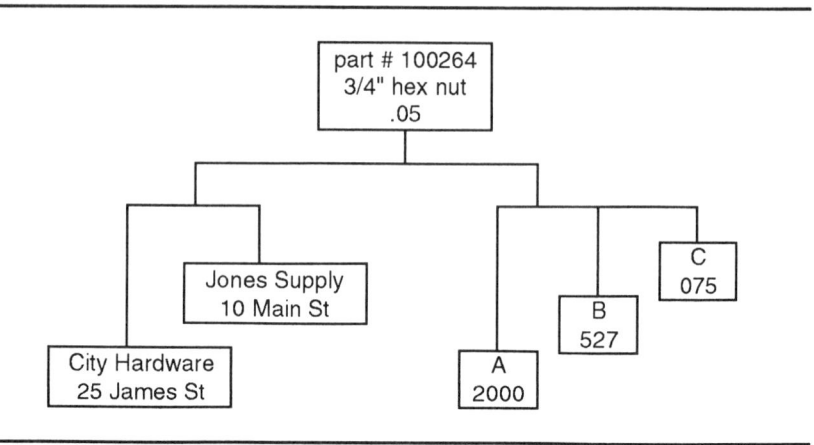

Figure 4.2. Example of IMS database record.

In Figure 4.2, note that there are more boxes than the structure in Figure 4.1 had. This is because IMS allows the application program (via DL/I instructions) to add additional segments that fit within the predefined structure. In this case, part number 100264 has two suppliers at present and is stocked in three warehouses. As suppliers are added or dropped, as warehouses are added or dropped, or inventory changes, the record dynamically expands or contracts. This was not possible before databases were available.

Partly because IMS databases resemble a family tree, you will encounter family terms used to describe the segments. Any segment that has subordinate segments (in our example, the part segment) is known as a *parent segment*. You've already guessed that the warehouse and supplier segments are *child segments*. To continue with the family-name format, the supplier and warehouse segments are called *sibling segments*. Where there are two of one segment type (e.g., Jones Supply and City hardware are both supplier segments), they are called *twin segments*. Finally, because the part segment is the highest segment in the structure, it is also known as a *root segment*. If you become involved with IMS systems, you will hear these terms regularly. You may also hear terms such as *logical child* or *logical parent*, but they're much too involved for this book.

As with other software that evolved in the MVS world, IMS requires that a company have a special technical staff to administer, tune, and support it. Defining a database for efficiency and good application performance is no easy task. Other features of IMS include facilities to recover data from power outages, system problems, and application errors. These are some of the reasons that many companies use complete packages such as IMS to oversee their applications.

Another feature of IMS is its online feature (IMS/DC, for IMS/Data Communications). Unlike TSO, which provided an online environment from which a skilled user could perform many functions, IMS/DC provides specific, business-oriented applications to be used by many people. This might include specific, company-developed programs for updating inventory or inquiring about customer account balances. Being designed to support predefined functions, IMS/DC can support many more terminal users than TSO and can also provide greater security with special passwords, if needed. You will usually find the programmers using TSO to develop applications and other company personnel using IMS/DC (or CICS, as we'll see later) to use the developed programs.

Terminal screens with IMS/DC (or CICS) are usually structured in a menu format, allowing the terminal user to select the function to be performed. Designing good screens can be important to ensuring an application is easily used. Using our previous example of a parts database, the company might develop programs for the following functions and have IMS/DC (or CICS) present a screen similar to the one in Figure 4.3.

Parts Management System

1. Add new part to inventory
2. Add/delete supplier to database
3. Change inventory for a part

Please select 1, 2, or 3. Press PF1 for help.
Press PF3 to terminate processing.

Figure 4.3. Example of online transaction screen.

On the screen in Figure 4.3, notice what is and isn't allowed. While often not documented by a company, transactions can be indicative of the authority of the terminal user. In this case, the person using this transaction is authorized to add new part descriptions, add or delete suppliers for a part, and keep the inventory up to date. What the person cannot do is delete a part. The fact that it is missing from the screen indicates that this function requires a higher authority and is probably done by a separate transaction.

IMS/DC uses the same DL/I communication technique described above but to provide instructions to IMS for sending and receiving information from terminals instead of reading and writing data to databases. Usually, when people refer to an IMS application, they mean it uses IMS for both terminal communication and for data administration.

Before leaving IMS, I should tell you that there are flaws in the example parts database I showed. The flaw (a database specialist could find more, I'm sure) is the use of *redundant data*. By redundant data I mean that some data will occur many times within the database. What makes this a problem is that it's almost impossible to keep it all accurate.

Let's review the sample database record in Figure 4.2. It shows that the address for City Hardware in the record for part number 100264 is 25 James St. Now, assume that the company that developed this parts inventory database has 20,000 parts in its manufacturing process. Assume also that 3,000 of them are available from City Hardware. With this structure, the name and address of City Hardware will appear 3,000 times in the database. That not only takes up space on DASD, but consider the complex database maintenance task if City Hardware were to move a few blocks away. Rather than just make one change to the database, someone would have to locate all 3,000 parts records and change each one.

Another observation is that the address of City Hardware has nothing to do with information on a specific part. I'll discuss that later when we get to DB2, although I wanted to point out here that most database integrity issues are shared by all database management systems.

While there are many different solutions to the problem of redundant data, one possibility is to separate the data into different databases and connect them so they appear as one database. (Note: When several IMS databases are structured to appear as one database, it is referred to as a logical database.) For our parts database, that might be the following:

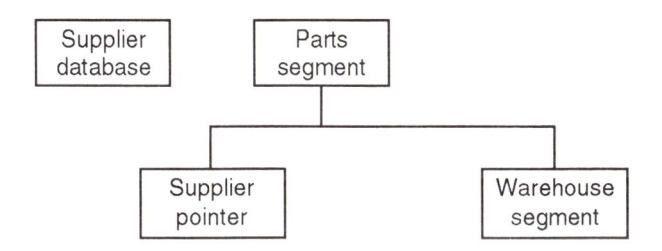

```
         ┌─────────┐    ┌─────────┐
         │Supplier │    │  Parts  │
         │database │    │ segment │
         └─────────┘    └────┬────┘
                             │
                    ┌────────┴────────┐
              ┌─────────┐       ┌──────────┐
              │Supplier │       │Warehouse │
              │ pointer │       │ segment  │
              └─────────┘       └──────────┘
```

Now, the supplier database, having only one segment for each supplier, is easy to keep current, and each supplier's address appears only once, not thousands of times. The parts database has a pointer to a supplier code number, allowing the database support specialists to make the application program "think" that all the information is in a single database.

It's not uncommon to see a database support staff at MVS installations ranging from about 20 to hundreds of specialists. Becoming an IMS (or CICS or DB2) specialist can be a challenging and rewarding career. For more information on IMS, I suggest you read QED's book, *IMS Design and Implementation Techniques* (see Chapter 7). It is not a programming manual but a book about the design and use of IMS for large-scale systems. I have worked with IMS since the mid-1970s and have high respect for this product. To me, IMS is the closest thing to being a "bullet-proof" product in MVS. Certainly, it is probably the most integrated software component within the MVS software set.

SECTION REVIEW

IMS has been around since the early 1970s and, for that reason, has matured into a highly reliable and useful software

82 THE MVS PRIMER

product. Companies use it to administer an entire application environment because of its administrative, support, and performance options. In most situations, IMS will outperform other software products in functions provided and in the volume of transactions processed per minute. Although it's been around for approximately 20 years, don't assume it is out of date.

4.3. CICS

CICS (Customer Information Control System, pronounced *kicks* by ardent fans and spelled out by others) has been growing in popularity for several years. IMS/DC was king in the 1970s and early 1980s, but CICS gets the attention now. One reason is its extensive flexibility and its ability to communicate with all IMS environments. Another is that it has continually expanded its capabilities and now can be combined with other products, including IMS. CICS is only a transaction manager and has no database structure of its own (although it does have the ability to read and write to VSAM files). You will often see hybrid structures where CICS is used. It might be a system where CICS controls terminal transactions and IMS/DB or DB2 is used for database access.

Because CICS is more flexible than IMS, it is also more complex (my opinion). While IMS's DL/I language is structured and allows only a few functions to be performed, CICS provides an extensive command language that makes it readily modified for new environments.

Like DL/I, CICS commands must be used from within another programming language. For example, to program a CICS transaction, a programmer might use COBOL and CICS commands. Unlike DL/I, which passed its requests to IMS through a traditional subprogram interface (the verb is CALL), CICS imbeds its commands directly within the programming language. Since CICS commands aren't known to the language compiler, you might wonder how CICS keeps from causing programming errors. Here is an example of a CICS command within a COBOL program to read from a file:

ONLINE ACCESS AND DATABASES   83

```
MOVE EMPLOYEE-ID TO FILE-READ-KEY
EXEC CICS READ DATASET('EMPFILE')
    INTO(EMPLOYEE-RECORD)
    RID-FLD(FILE-READ-KEY)
END-EXEC
MOVE EMPLOYEE-NAME TO PRINT-RECORD
```

If you're familiar with COBOL, you know that the statements on the second through fifth lines aren't COBOL statements and will cause a compiler error. CICS solves this by using a preprocessor program to create COBOL statements *before* the program is read by the COBOL compiler. (The process of using a preprocessor is also used by programs with imbedded DB2 commands, covered later.). See Figure 4.4 for an example of the steps to compile a CICS program.

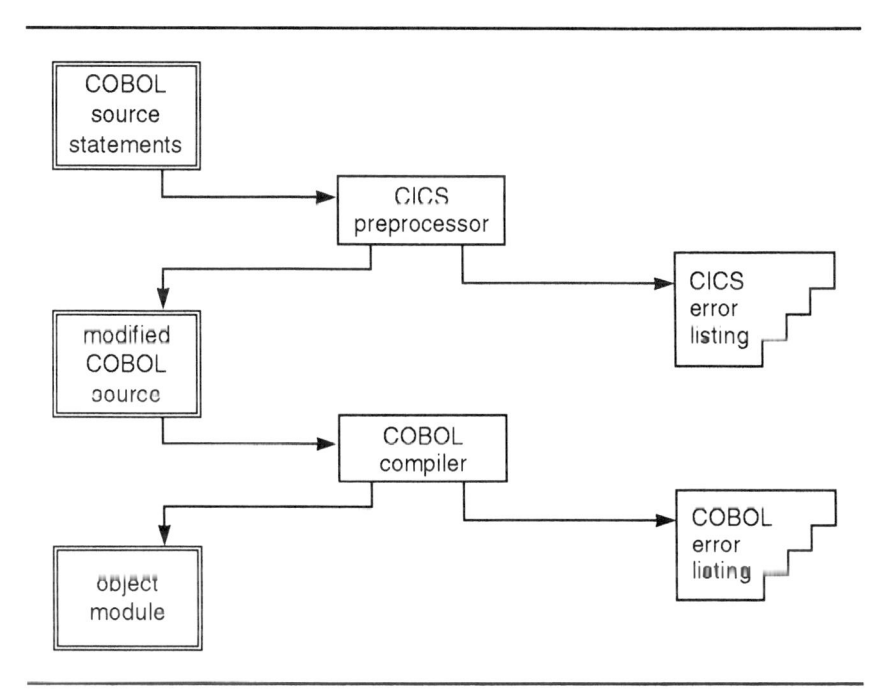

Figure 4.4. Example of CICS and COBOL compile steps.

In Figure 4.4, you can see that the programmer must cope with getting by two obstacles, the COBOL compiler AND the CICS preprocessor. The CICS preprocessor will report any errors in coding CICS commands (CICS commands always begin with EXEC CICS and always end with END-EXEC) and will convert properly coded CICS commands to COBOL equivalents. Actually, this is a blessing because this ensures to the programmer that both CICS and COBOL statements were coded correctly. With IMS and DL/I, the programmer never knew if DL/I statements were coded correctly until the program was tested.

In several instances, I have referenced both IMS/DC and CICS. That is because, to a large degree, both provide similar services for presenting applications to users. To the terminal user, there is little if any difference. Your company is probably using one, or both, of these products. Regardless of the one used, these software products greatly extend the power of MVS.

SECTION REVIEW

Frankly, CICS is fun for programmers because of its flexibility. The control of processes and terminal screens is extensive, and it can be combined with IMS or DB2 databases, if needed.

4.4. DB2 AND SQL

DB2 (I think IBM prefers that we say DATABASE 2, but most of us shorten it to DB2) and SQL (Structured Query Language, pronounced *sequel*) have grown in popularity among the programming profession in recent years. One reason is that SQL is a programming language that runs on many different computers, even PCs. This common language appeals to companies wanting to develop applications across many environments. First, let's clarify some terms.

DB2 is the name of IBM's implementation of a relational database facility on MVS systems and not a generic description of SQL or relational databases. An MVS DB2 relational database is accessed through SQL commands, but just because a particular database is accessed with SQL commands does not mean it is a DB2 database. (For example, if you used SQL to access a relational database on a PC, it would not be a DB2 database.) DB2, then, is a database management system. SQL is a relational access language that works within a given database management system.

Where IMS used hierarchical data structures, DB2 uses relational data structures. Relational structures are more flexible than hierarchical ones, but this technology was the last to evolve of the products discussed in this chapter. IMS and TSO were sufficiently efficient to allow their use on IBM mainframes even back in the 1970s. DB2, on the other hand, needed the more powerful mainframes available today before it could be as effective as it is proving to be. Also, DB2 is considerably more efficient now than it was years ago.

As with CICS, the use of SQL statements within a formal programming language, such as COBOL, requires a preprocessor (see Figure 4.4) to translate the SQL statements into COBOL statements. As with CICS, the statements are preceded by EXEC SQL and followed by END-EXEC.

Relational data structures are intuitively obvious (at least the simple ones are). Whenever you use a table of information, whether it is an airline schedule, an income tax table, or a menu in a sub shop, you can easily use the data. (What? You've never been to a sub shop? I guess in some places these sandwiches are called *grinders* or *heros* or *hoagies*. In upstate New York, we call them submarine sandwiches or just "subs.") Figure 4.5 shows an example of a typical on-the-wall menu.

The menu is a relational database (sort of). You can determine the price of a whole salami sandwich in Figure 4.5 by reading down the *rows* of sandwich options and then reading across the *columns* of prices. You easily determine that the price is $4.20. In other words, you located the data element and price by relating the desired row element to the desired column element. That's how relational data structures work. The more complex structures join multiple tables together for the search.

86 THE MVS PRIMER

Sandwiches	Half Sub	Whole Sub	Super Sub
Regular	2.50	3.85	4.50
Turkey	2.60	4.10	4.65
Meatball	2.85	4.50	5.00
Salami	2.60	4.20	4.60
Capicola	2.75	3.95	4.75
Options			
Peppers	.10	.20	.25
Onions	.05	.10	.13
Cheese	.05	.10	.15

Figure 4.5. Example of relational data structure.

By joining the two menus (sandwiches and options), you can easily figure the cost of a particular sandwich if peppers and/or onions are added. Relational databases may be joined together when they have like components.

Since MVS systems tend to have large databases, the rows and columns in a DB2 database can require extensive computing capacity to locate the desired data element. This requirement is being overshadowed by the flexible data structures and also by the query-oriented software products that allow nonprogrammers to access information.

A strong issue of designing DB2 databases is called *normalization*. This refers to the process, usually done by database specialists at a company, of organizing the data based on its relationship to other data. Properly normalized data (a topic far too complex for this book) have a predictable relationship to other data. For example, a data segment containing employee name and employee age would be proper, because an employee has only one name and one age. If we wanted variable information (such as information about courses the employee has taken, prior job titles, or prior salary changes), it would not be appropriate to place this variable information in the data segment for employee name and age. There are many other rules of normalizing data (called *normal forms*), and the subject is nontrivial.

In addition to the SQL and DB2 products, IBM also offers a companion product, QMF (Query Management Facility). I find this product exciting because it allows programmers and nonprogrammers to enter DB2 queries interactively from a terminal. This hands-on feature makes corporate information immediately available without writing application programs.

I recall that the first QMF query in which I participated gave a vice-president some marketing information that he had never expected. We were demonstrating a new DB2 system to him at the time. Instead of waiting for the end of the demonstration, he asked us to print the screen information to a local printer, and he ran from the room, clutching the sheet of paper. Such excitement you don't get from batch reports. Why? Because batch reports usually produce data that was anticipated.

Although I present the concept in simple terms, DB2, SQL, and QMF require expertise to use effectively. I have experience as a project manager who participated in installing a DB2 system, but I do not have hands-on experience to share with you. Instead, I suggest you pursue some other books that address the full scope of SQL and DB2. QED has books for the application programmer and for the project manager or system designer (see Chapter 7). I know of no other publisher who offers such an extensive set of publications addressing this emerging technology.

SECTION REVIEW

DB2 has its roots in more academic areas than other software products. Relational database theory is complex, and it took IBM many years to develop a product that could implement it as DB2 has. Products such as DB2 were not feasible prior to MVS.

CHAPTER REVIEW

This chapter presented information that many people do not associate with MVS, such as databases and transaction managers. I included it because it is software such as this that is routinely part of most MVS configurations. Understanding the

88 THE MVS PRIMER

concepts of these products does not prepare you to use them, but I hope you have a better feeling about the depth of MVS services and appreciate why so many large companies feel that, even with the skills and support requirements imposed by MVS, MVS is worth the investment.

For years, I have heard comments such as "the mainframe is dead." Don't believe it. Yes, PCs and other forms of smaller, distributed hardware will do much in the future to improve our use of corporate facilities, but one of the major reasons distributed hardware is useful is that MVS and a mainframe data center provide centralized support and access.

VOCABULARY REVIEW

The terms addressed in this chapter are important to you if your company uses, or plans to use, these extended components of MVS. These are the components of MVS that are the most popular today, and you need to be familiar with the concepts presented. These are also some of the acronyms most frequently listed in resumes and in classified job advertisements.

TSO

CICS

IMS

DB2

DL/I

QMF

redundant data

relational data

hierarchical data

The time: Thursday morning, 1:00 A.M.

The location: The data center master operator console

"Working here as an operator is really great. When I finished high school, I didn't know what to do. Taking the job here as an operator trainee has been super. Oh, the hours aren't great. Some weeks I work all night, and some weeks I work all day. With a constantly changing schedule, it's hard to adjust my personal life, but it's a lot better than working nights full time.

"To be honest, though, there's a special quality about the night shift. I turn the lights down a bit in the console area, and then I turn the lights in the DASD farm completely out. It's an eerie feeling, having only a few of us in this massive building, but most processes are fully automated now. I don't know what it was like in the 'old days,' but I can do everything I need to from this one console. No, one console doesn't mean a single terminal and keyboard. My console has 16 terminals and even more keyboards. They're stacked in rows above my head, and each terminal gives me information about a specific subsystem (I noticed earlier tonight that the CICS response-time problem seems to have been solved).

"One thing I especially like is that, on night shift, everyone seems friendlier. Last week, the department vice-president stopped in wearing some scruffy jeans and sneaks and brought us some coffee and snacks. It's nice to feel appreciated. Sometimes programmers come in from home to fix problems, and they're always appreciative of our assistance. If there's a better job in this world, I haven't found it.

"Excuse me, I see some messages from MVS coming up on the primary console. It looks like we lost the communications line to London. That's a priority one situation here, so I must alert our on-duty systems programmer and call our on-call staff. I often wonder what it's like to be called out of bed in the middle of the night. That's got to be tough. This night's going to be interesting...

"Oh, one more thing. You'll have to leave now. Guests aren't allowed in the data center during priority situations. Good night."

5

MVS Today

This chapter will not attempt to present new information (well, not much), but it will focus on how the various components have matured into today's processing environment. What you have read in previous chapters holds true today, but there are subtle differences to share.

5.1. MVS VARIATIONS

When you read or hear about different MVS versions, it is still one product, MVS. The suffix of SP, XA, or ESA identifies to what level the particular MVS has been upgraded. It's very much like buying a car and adding options. Whereas MVS might be considered the standard model, the SP version adds fuel injection, the XA version includes dual exhausts and a racing transmission, and the ESA version adds a supercharger and can do wheelies in the parking lot (well, sort of).

Seriously, what provides these upgrade options is that IBM has integrated functionality into both the hardware and the software. The more powerful versions of MVS incorporate some functions in microcode, which executes much faster. By delegating some software functions to hardware, the computer can process applications more quickly. Here is an elementary (and I do mean elementary) review of the various levels of MVS. For more specifics, see the publications in Chapter 7 from IBM.

92 THE MVS PRIMER

MVS is the basic version. Everything discussed in this book is provided by the basic level of MVS. To most programmers (except those that are involved in special situations), this is all they need to know. MVS became the standard because it provided not only addressability to 16 million bytes of memory for all active jobs, but 16 million bytes of memory to *each* job. Providing multiple virtual storage address spaces eliminated the competition for memory among various jobs in the system. (Reminder: An address space in MVS is the total available virtual memory that can be allocated to each active job.)

MVS/SP was the first upgrade for MVS that used microcode for some functions. Totally transparent to applications, this extended the lifespan of a mainframe. The benefit it provided was speed.

MVS/XA is considered the current MVS standard. It is different from previous versions of MVS primarily because it can use a 31-bit address (prior versions used only a 24-bit address). While 24-bit machines could access up to 16 million bytes of memory, XA can access up to 2 billion bytes — a substantial leap in capability. This increased an address space 128 times over that of previous versions while still providing the same basic services as MVS or MVS/SP. The concept of MVS/XA is similar to the example in Figure 3.6, except that it provides 2 gigabytes of addressable storage to each active job instead of only 16 megabytes. This need for more memory was dictated by the gradually increasing capability and function of both IBM software and customer applications. This benefit is not automatic. While MVS/XA can provide the facility, application programs need to be recompiled with a language compiler that supports 31-bit addressing (e.g., Assembler H for assembler applications, COBOL II for COBOL applications).

MVS/ESA, the latest upgrade in the MVS line, extends memory use beyond current levels, allowing applications not only to use memory for applications but also for in-memory data spaces. This use of memory for what was once exclusive to DASD is indicative of the change in how memory is used. Until now, memory was always considered the most expensive resource to a data center. Now, it is viewed as an excellent medium to store data for online systems. This allows a multidimensional use of system resources, as shown in Figure 5.1. Each job may use one complete set of addressable virtual memory for program logic and additional sets for data storage.

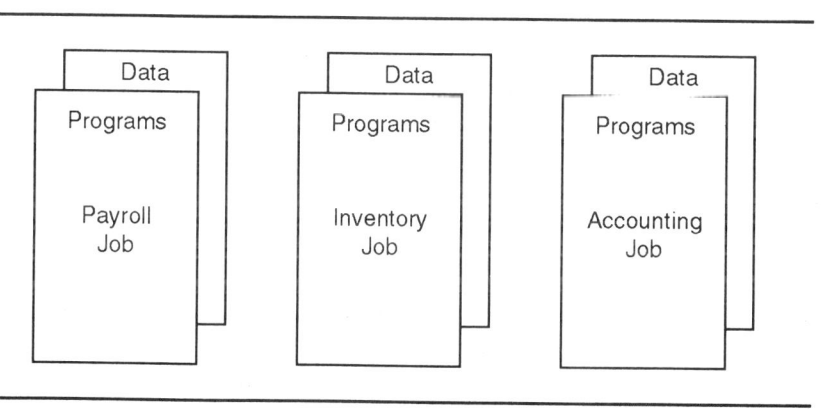

```
+------------------+     +------------------+     +------------------+
|     Data         |     |     Data         |     |     Data         |
|   Programs       |     |   Programs       |     |   Programs       |
|                  |     |                  |     |                  |
|    Payroll       |     |   Inventory      |     |   Accounting     |
|      Job         |     |      Job         |     |      Job         |
+------------------+     +------------------+     +------------------+
```

Figure 5.1. Example of multiple ESA address spaces.

Additional benefits of MVS/ESA promise extended availability of the mainframe. This is done via multiprocessing, where several processors share a common task, and Sysplex (for *Systems Complex*), where several processors are interconnected to be a logical computer complex. In a Sysplex structure, if a processor fails, others can pick up the processing responsibilities. This is similar to backup facilities on an airplane, where one instrument or component can replace a damaged one without requiring intervention. See Figure 5.2 for an example.

MVS/ESA will continue to expand in the future as MVS incorporates additional functions for enterprise support. IBM has announced versions of IMS and CICS that bear the ESA suffix. Watch for it to happen, in time, at your shop.

94 THE MVS PRIMER

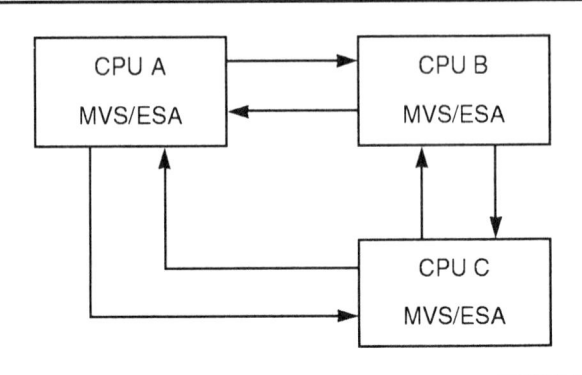

```
       ┌──────────┐        ┌──────────┐
       │  CPU A   │───────▶│  CPU B   │
       │ MVS/ESA  │◀───────│ MVS/ESA  │
       └──────────┘        └──────────┘
            ▲                   │ ▲
            │                   ▼ │
            │              ┌──────────┐
            └─────────────▶│  CPU C   │
                           │ MVS/ESA  │
                           └──────────┘
```

Figure 5.2. Example of a Sysplex structure.

SECTION REVIEW

Okay, so this wasn't a big section, and maybe you don't care about this stuff. My goal was to make you aware of the integration of hardware and software and the ability of a data center to upgrade from one version of MVS to another. If you got all that, you're on target. The future of MVS is with MVS/ESA.

5.2. MVS COMPONENTS

Today, you will normally find many components that were never before used at the same data center combined for more flexibility. As technology expanded, and as application languages became more dependent on each other, it was obvious (?) that they would not remain separate. For example, once upon a time, a data center would not use both CICS and IMS/DC. Now it is common because there are applications and benefits from each.

This integration has caused many additional software products to emerge, most of which we don't need to know about in this book. They were developed to provide data and application integrity as applications use multiple environments concurrently (for example, both CICS and IMS/DC). This book will not address such technical elements, but you should at least be aware of their existence. (Reminder: when you hear a new acronym, always ask for the definition and the purpose of the new software.) This chapter will highlight some new activities that are affecting MVS data centers now and in the future.

5.2.1. Data repository

You may have heard about the repository. IBM already provides a data dictionary product, a product that keeps track of data elements and where they are used in applications. The repository is intended to provide extensive enhancements to corporate control and use of data, plus provide support for information on business activities and goals, application systems, and relationships between each of these activities. If the repository is at your company, or will be soon, I suggest you read QED's *IBM's Repository Manager/MVS* (Chapter 7). It contains extensive information on this major new IBM product.

5.2.2. Distributed data

Until recently, most corporate data was stored on the mainframe. Now, MVS supports a new telecommunications protocol (called LU 6.2, where LU stands for Logical Unit and comes from IBM's Systems Network Architecture, SNA). Prior to LU 6.2, applications used an earlier protocol, LU 2.0.

The LU 2.0 protocol was easy to understand because it treated mainframes as mainframes and terminals (PCs) as terminals. Data was moved from one to the other by what is known as uploads and downloads. By that, I mean that software copied data from one device to another but did no other processing on the data. LU 2.0 is similar to putting data in an envelope and mailing it somewhere. Nothing happens to the data during transit. When I write software at home and upload it to a company's mainframe, I am using the LU 2.0 protocol. When companies moved data from corporate data centers to remote offices, it was with the LU 2.0 protocol.

Now, while most companies aren't using it yet, LU 6.2 works more like a telephone call than like mail. It allows a remote workstation and a mainframe to interact, passing data as needed. This new technique is supported in IMS/DC and in

CICS and promises to provide more powerful applications in the future where the terminal user is using a PC for a workstation. It will also allow a company to store data where the data is usually needed instead of always putting it with the mainframe. (For example, in my family, my sister is the family historian. If I need to know an uncle's birthday, I call her for the information instead of asking her to mail her entire collection of family history to me. That's distributed processing. It's cheaper and more efficient.) IBM is implementing LU 6.2 under the auspices of the software product, APPC/MVS (Advanced Program-to-Program Communication). This enhancement will tie MVS mainframes to PC desktops and remote non-MVS, mid-size computers. If your company has many remote sites, this may be in your future. For an example, see Figure 5.3.

In Figure 5.3, PS/2 represents IBM's desktop workstations running the OS/2 software, and AS/400 represents IBM's mid-size AS/400 computer running the OS/400 software. Tying different computers of different sizes into one network allows small offices, large warehouses and plants, and the home office all to share access to the same systems and data.

5.2.3. IMS, DB2, and CICS integration

In previous chapters, you got the feeling that each of the major products (IMS, DB2, CICS) worked independently, but this is no longer true. In today's world, many data centers use all three products. Furthermore, the products now talk to each

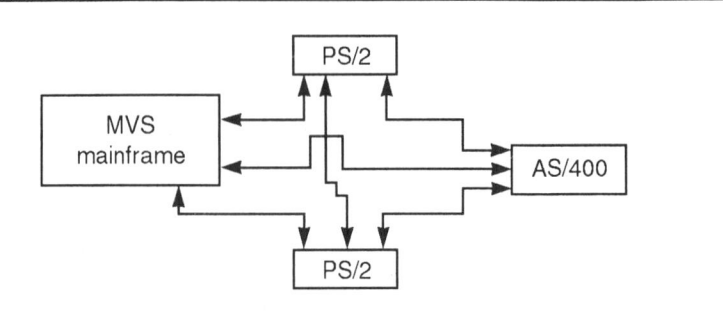

Figure 5.3. Example of APPC with SNA network.

other and provide enhanced systems capability. IBM's current software capabilities allow a company to pick the database manager of choice and the transaction manager of choice separately. This flexibility allows project managers to assess the benefits of the various systems and use whatever fits best. A far cry from the mid-1970s when a project manager had to use whatever was available.

As Figure 5.4 shows, the components of MVS can now be connected together for more effective processing, providing more options in building user applications.

5.2.4. The role of assembler language

Many people, including programmers, feel that assembler language is dead. After all, why write in byte-oriented languages that are machine-dependent when you can use higher-level languages? The answer is simple. Assembler language provides the putty to keep the other components working properly. It is because assembler speaks the language of the hardware that makes it a powerful tool, not despite it. In many complex situations, the only systems solution is to use assembler to tell the computer what is required when high-level languages are unable to do so.

Although assembler language is no longer appropriate for general applications development, it remains a key factor in maintaining computer foundations for major applications. If I

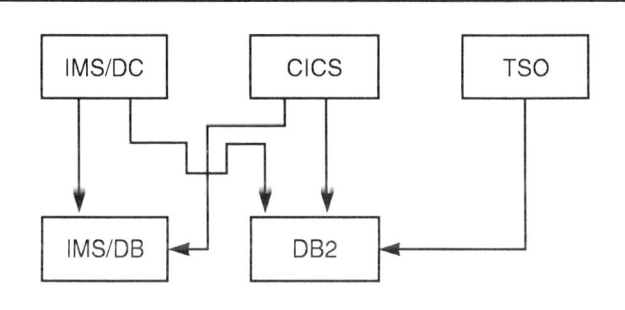

Figure 5.4. Example of shared IMS, CICS, and DB2 system.

98 THE MVS PRIMER

were to name my favorite language, it would be assembler. Why? Because it lets me have maximum freedom in using the computer for any given solution. Some people argue that assembler should never be used. I reply that, when needed, there are no alternatives. For an example of assembler language, see Figure 5.5.

```
JOBID          CSECT
*   Locate JOB name and STEP name
*   Written by David Shelby Kirk, 1991
JOBID          AMODE  31
JOBID          RMODE  ANY
R1             EQU    1
R2             EQU    2
R5             EQU    5
R6             EQU    6
R7             EQU    7
R10            EQU    10
R11            EQU    11
R12            EQU    12
R13            EQU    13
R14            EQU    14
R15            EQU    15
               SAVE   (14,12),,*
               USING  JOBID,R12
               LR     R12,R15
               LR     R11,R13
               LA     R13,SAVEAREA
               ST     R13,8(0,R11)
               ST     R11,4(0,R13)
               LR     R5,R1
               GETMAIN R,LV=8
               LR     R6,R1
               GETMAIN R,LV=ENDADDR-EXTLIST+4
               LR     R7,R1
               MVC    0(ENDADDR-EXTLIST,R7),EXTLIST
               EXTRACT (6),MF=(E,(7))
               L      R6,0(,R6)
               L      R2,0(,R5)
               MVC    0(16,R2),0(R6)
               L      R13,SAVEAREA+4
               RETURN (14,12),RC=0
SAVEAREA       DC     18F'0'
EXTLIST        EXTRACT FIELDS=TIOT,MF=L
ENDADDR        EQU    *
               END    JOBID
```

Figure 5.5. Example of assembler program.

Messy, isn't it? Very efficient, and loved by those who write in it, assembler language can be frightening to casual readers. Perhaps, that is why it has fallen from favor, but for all the wrong reasons.

5.2.5. Packaging of access methods

MVS now packages several support products, including access methods and the sort facility (DFSORT) under the umbrella of Data Facility Product (MVS/DFP). When you see a reference to DFP or MVS/DFP, it involves what we covered in prior chapters on access methods, catalog services, and utility functions.

SECTION REVIEW

This section didn't present all of the components of MVS. If it did, the book would be much larger and not of interest to most readers. Instead, these are the evolving components that you will most frequently encounter as you work with MVS. Much of what is discussed here may already be in use at your company.

I also wanted to sensitize you to the fact that you will need to reevaluate your perception of MVS components from time to time. Some professionals, for example, think IMS is obsolete because it has been around for 20 years or so. Not so. IMS is still a major component of MVS and continues to improve as it provides extended services. Companies using MVS and its many components have invested millions of dollars in their systems. No one, certainly not IBM, wants to remove any service that users need.

CHAPTER REVIEW

My goal in presenting this chapter is to emphasize that MVS continues to evolve. You need to be familiar with these components that will grow in importance as MVS grows. As corporate processing continues to expand away from the mainframe, the mainframe's ability to support the processing requirements will expand. Distributed processing, the data repository, and the combining of functions among the major software components will provide many job opportunities and corporate challenges throughout the 1990s.

(While I have no crystal ball, nor any inside information from IBM, I would not be surprised to see the MVS's name change within a few years. As always, the name is derived from the services that were most important at the time. In the 1960s, MVT represented that the computer could do several tasks concurrently. In the 1970s, SVS boasted a system that had virtual storage. In the 1980s, MVS was the system with multiple virtual storage. As the features of the operating system continue to multiply, it seems only logical that a new name must come.)

VOCABULARY REVIEW

Terms introduced in this chapter are MVS's future. Become familiar with them, and look for them in other books, magazines, and texts. As MVS becomes more widely distributed, these terms will become more commonplace. Being familiar with how they fit in the MVS infrastructure can only help you.

MVS/ESA

APPC/MVS

SNA

COBOL II

PS/2

AS/400

Repository Manager/MVS

MVS/DFP

Sysplex

The time: Friday afternoon, 3:00 P.M.

The location: The MIS Director's office

"Sure, I like being the director. The job has prestige, pays well, and I worked hard to get here. I admit it isn't as much fun as programming was, but somebody has to run the department, and I feel, with my background in programming and operations, I am more sensitive to the needs of our employees than some others might be.

"Okay, I admit that we had to cut the training budget this year, and some of the programmers are still using 10-year-old terminals. I didn't say that I was God; I said I was the director. It's tough to keep up to date in technology, keep costs down for users, provide challenges for the staff, meet the budget, and stay aware of industry shifts and hardware market value.

"For example, our IBM 3090 is three years old. We have the option to upgrade it, sell it for a larger model, or buy a second mainframe and integrate the two. None of these choices is easy, and the financial burden is all new to me. If I can convince some users to change their requirements, our current model can get the work done for another year, but then the market value will have dropped again. Which is the better choice? If we upgrade our version of MVS, we'll get more throughput, but at what price? The benefits are there, but we'll need to upgrade our applications to use the new techniques. What will that cost?

"Finally, in addition to trying to manage this data center, the CEO complains that I need to spend more time 'learning the business.' If I could just increase a day from 24 hours to 40, I think things would be easier to handle.

"Excuse me while I call home to say I'll be late for dinner again. This will be the third time this week. Thank God we have the weekend together."

6

Learning MVS

You have probably decided by now that learning MVS is not a simple process. A classroom course of a day or two just won't do it. Learning MVS takes time, first learning one skill and gaining familiarity with its syntax and benefits and then learning another skill. MVS is an exciting and challenging computer environment, and mastery of it takes time.

As with any new skill, the learning itself is part of the benefit of knowing it. If you work in an MVS environment, plot out your personal training program, and, most of all, give yourself time to enjoy the experience. I've been learning MVS for over 20 years, and I can probably list as much that I don't know as I do know. If you want to master a complete environment quickly, MVS isn't for you. If you enjoy continuous learning, you'll love it. But you must take the initiative and the accountability. Company training programs provide a service, but please don't blame them if you aren't learning. Only you can make it happen.

What I have constructed in this chapter are suggested skills for theoretical job titles. You may find them helpful if you're building a training program at your company, or you just may get some ideas for your own growth.

There are a variety of training media available for MVS topics, and your company can advise you on what is available.

From my personal experience in training programmers for the last 25+ years, here are my impressions.

- Classroom training: With the right instructor, this is the best. Yes, it costs more, but the interaction of students with each other and the positive reenforcement are major benefits. An instructor with vision can inspire students. No other media comes close.

- Books: Yes, this is my second choice. If you can't have a personal instructor, you will usually find that, regardless of the subject matter, the printed word is the most up-to-date information on any topic. Also, you will need to build a personal reference library anyway.

- CBT: Computer-based training has taken its knocks, sometimes justified, sometimes not. I like it. A good CBT course can ensure that you have the proper survival skills. If your company also provides a tutor to give the personal touch, all the better. Some of the newer ones have interactive video, providing a multimedia environment that can accelerate the learning process.

- Video courses: I rate video courses last, not because of poor quality but because they are often misused. These are great for conceptual knowledge and can accomplish this goal more economically than other methods. Also, a company can make an extensive number of topics available quickly with a video approach. They can be effective for technical topics, but success requires that a course tutor be available to help students with the assignments. Unfortunately, this assistance is often lacking because some companies let the video training library just sit on the shelf. With a coordinator and, ideally, group sessions, video training can minimize the need for the coordinator to be a polished instructor. This can be cost-effective if the video courses are current.

Again, unfortunately, some companies buy video training programs and keep them far beyond their useful life. If not current, courses can do more harm than good. Classroom courses are less likely to be outdated (although it still happens too often), and CBT courses are usually too new to have this problem. I mention it here with video training only because the video approach has been with us for 20+ years. Don't misunderstand me. I have happily signed contracts for large video training programs and felt it was money well spent. I'm reminding you to fit the media to the need. Any media works best if a tutor can participate and relate the general information to how your company actually uses the product and to give direct feedback to a student. Video training is inexpensive, but it isn't cost-effective (nor is any other media) if the human element is ignored.

6.1. MVS PROGRAMMER SKILL REQUIREMENTS

Being a programmer in an MVS environment requires a special set of skills, but the matrix depends on the specific shop. In addition to knowing a programming language that is used in MVS (Assembler, COBOL, FORTRAN, PL/1, C), the programmer needs to know how to navigate through various MVS services and how to use various standard tools that are available. (Most MVS shops have TSO and ISPF. Knowing those two products is essential.) Normal career skills, such as structured programming and structured design, are omitted from this list.

Admittedly, some of my comments about employers may seem rather harsh. It is not my intent to disparage them, but I want to encourage the employee to take control and not rely on others to provide the training you need. Some companies provide outstanding training programs — some provide none. If you are with a company that has no training programs, you can still pursue your own education and achieve your objectives.

Here are my suggestions:

For MVS survival skills

Build a solid foundation on the basics. That means JCL, the Linkage Editor, and utilities. Regardless of what else you learn, you will always benefit from a solid grasp of these building blocks. Don't rely on company training either. Learning JCL from scratch is easily a five-day course, and your company may attempt to do it in three or four hours (yes, I've seen it done — often). If you get the opportunity to attend a classroom course, by all means do so. But take what you hear with a grain of salt. Some JCL courses oversimplify the very mechanics that you want to master. Also, buy yourself a good reference text so that you will have the information readily available.

Don't try to master these skills in one sitting or in one course. JCL is best learned by taking it a step at a time. As you become comfortable with one topic or technique, go back to your text and study another. Give yourself a year or so to learn the skills and develop a personal road map to follow.

For language skills

While you may have learned a programming language at college or elsewhere, don't assume it matches the MVS equivalent. MVS languages typically provide extensive services that are not available on college or business school computers. Your old college textbook often will not be sufficient. Invest in a book developed for professionals, not one developed for students.

Again, if a course is available, take it. Be sensitive, though, to the fact that many language courses are taught by people who learned the language 10 or more years ago. If they have not kept pace with the language, you may be learning programming practices that are years out of date. (While it may surprise you, I often encounter trainers who teach programming techniques that have been obsolete for two decades. I also see such techniques in textbooks.)

For programming and debugging skills

Learning the basic online interactive tools will be a benefit. TSO and ISPF are the most common and, while they are often listed in job descriptions, many programmers know no more about TSO than they do about the sex life of a housefly. That isn't a criticism. In most cases, there is little need to know TSO commands, simply because ISPF eliminates the need.

Also, "knowing ISPF" at most shops means just being able to use the text editor in some rudimentary fashion to modify or enter source code. Again, acquiring a book on the subject immediately raises you head and shoulders above a large percentage of other programmers. Courses on these topics are rarely presented. Why? Because most programmers can grasp the basics by just using it. ISPF is a great product as you will see once you use it. At many companies, ISPF is taught before JCL (or instead of it). If so, take the training as offered, but you should still follow up with the JCL and Linkage Editor training mentioned above.

For specialized skills

Beyond the basics, you will need to pursue special books or courses. Learning IMS, DB2, or CICS requires that you devote time to grasping the fundamentals of the respective environments. If you decide to wait until someone else trains you, you may have a long wait, depending on the employer. You will usually benefit by taking the initiative yourself. You will get more out of a training course on these topics if you have already done some research and reading.

6.2. MVS ANALYST SKILL REQUIREMENTS

Analysts face a dilemma. Because they are often considered to be nontechnical, they are given little opportunity to learn about MVS, using only pencil and paper to do their jobs. On the other hand, the data they need to analyze are often available only through MVS services. My recommendation is to learn TSO and ISPF so you can access MVS facilities, learn JCL so you can use various software utility programs, and then learn about the major components (e.g., IMS, CICS, DB2). Then you can make realistic judgments about their appropriateness for a given application.

A good analyst should feel comfortable using a terminal connected to MVS. Becoming proficient requires that you learn what skills the programmers use and use them yourself. A suggestion: Share your training desires with a few programmers you know. Most will respond positively to the opportunity to share their skills with you. A word of caution: They may present too much, too quickly, in their enthusiasm. Attempt to guide the training sessions to real situations you face, not theoretical possibilities. Take notes.

6.3. MVS MIS MANAGER SKILL REQUIREMENTS

I still encounter managers who believe their job is just to manage programmers and analysts and operators, having no awareness of the work environment that the staff faces each day. To maintain the respect of employees, you need to be able to recognize MVS components, make decisions on which ones to use, and ensure that affected personnel are properly trained to use the components. That means you need some technical training yourself (probably reading).

I say *probably* reading because there are so few courses available to help a manager make decisions about products. There are many that teach all the mechanics, but few that help managers do their jobs.

Here are my suggestions:

1. Read this book twice, maybe three times. You first need a firm foundation on the terms, the acronyms, what connects to what, and what each major component does. You could get the same information by attending a variety of "management workshops," but you have little time. If you must go off-site for training, reserve the time for more specialized training.

2. Next, take a couple of programmers to lunch. They will enjoy the experience, you will learn a bit of office gossip, and they can give you feedback on your perceptions about MVS and on what skills they think are important at your shop. If they are unaware of some of the terms you have learned, it may indicate a training issue. Do this three times and take notes. Note: If you are a senior manager, don't make the mistake of taking middle managers to lunch instead. I was one once. We will use the opportunity to sell you on our preferences. Programmers will give you better feedback.

3. Next, if you're a middle manager, take a couple of analysts to lunch. Get their perspective on what benefits they see in

using DB2, IMS, or whatever component interests you. Their feedback may give you additional direction that complements what the programmers told you, or it may indicate that the analysts would benefit from training, too. If you are a senior manager, call a meeting of your managers to discuss technology directions and ask for suggestions. The joint meeting should give you feedback on preferred directions. The managers may have been waiting for years for the opportunity to recommend a move to newer technology and are usually very positive about such a meeting.

4. Now, take a couple of systems programmers to lunch. They'll be surprised by your interest, they may toss more acronyms at you than I covered in this book, and they may make you feel the effort isn't worth it. Persist. Systems programmers usually know more about what is available or what could be done. Take notes.

5. Now, review the book list in Chapter 7. The QED books will be all-encompassing. The IBM books will be more specific. You will benefit by a mix of both. I have read each one listed. I get no kickback from either vendor and have nothing to gain here. If yours is a large shop and you are up to date on MVS, I suggest you read the QED book on the Repository Manager, as it also includes information on many new IBM directions. If your shop is new to DB2 or considering acquiring it, the two DB2 books can be valuable assets. There are several books listed from IBM for managers, and those that relate to your environment will prove useful.

6. After doing some reading, do a "sanity check" with your clients. If they watch technology, they will be encouraged about your concerns. If they have been concerned with the budget too long, they may discourage you from contemplating making data more available, providing better management services, or developing better online systems. If so, you may want to arrange some constructive training that you can jointly attend. By going together, you place yourself on an even footing with them, and the outcome is usually positive.

7. By now, you know more about MVS, about technology, about what directions are possible than many of your peers. And it wasn't difficult, was it? Your next step — and I can't help you here — is to ensure that you are close to the business needs and can suggest technology that is appropriate. Being appropriate is always more useful than just being new. Good luck.

6.4. MVS END USER SKILL REQUIREMENTS

To the end user, who is blamed for everything about poor systems, I encourage you first to develop a conceptual knowledge of the components available at your company. If your company uses DB2 but not IMS, don't waste your time learning IMS. It's doubtful that any project you want done with IMS would justify the expense of acquiring and installing it. Stick to what your MIS staff knows.

On the other hand, if your company uses few (or none) of the MVS components identified in this book, then you may want to voice some concerns about it. Most MIS departments want to stay current with technology. When they don't, it's often because they assume budgetary concerns won't justify adding the power of a database. Used appropriately, newer technology should help you do your job better, and MIS should be able to help you do it.

If your MIS department is trying to be more responsive to user needs (and most are), tell the department manager of your desire to develop more knowledge of MIS technology, and you should get all the assistance (and maybe more) that you need. Most MIS people are only too happy to share their information with an interested user.

6.5. SUGGESTED READING APPROACH

If you expected this book to suggest that television, movies, or other media would be more informative than the printed word, then you're overlooking the biases of an author. Besides, books are great for doorstops or pressing flowers, and they fill up book shelves much better than bric-a-brac.

Seriously, if you are planning a career in any topic, you will want to build a reference library. With a good book, you can always pick it up to review a particular topic. With other media, it's not so easy. Most MVS topics are so complex that you will do best by having a ready reference for problem assistance and a ready index to easily identify new skills.

Check the various manuals in Chapter 7. If you already know the technical environment in which you will work, the selection of the appropriate books should be easy. If you're not sure, give yourself a few weeks to learn the basics and then make some decisions. You can then pick IBM manuals for specifics and personal books where a more complete exposure is desired.

CHAPTER REVIEW

Okay, so maybe I seemed a bit harsh toward employer training programs. As I said earlier, that is not my intent. You, and only you, are accountable for your education. Some companies provide an excellent, well-balanced program. Others, even when that is their goal, fall short. Having the skill to train programmers is a special talent, and just because people want to do it doesn't mean they can. That doesn't detract from the employer's intent. This is an area where you can take charge of your own future.

The time: Saturday afternoon, 2:00 P.M.

The location: The beach

"Of all weekends to be assigned the 'beeper' and to be on-call for system problems, this has to be the worst. Here I finally meet the greatest guy, and he invites me to spend the afternoon at the beach with him and his daughter. I had been wanting to get to know her better so we could be friends, and here I am feeling nervous with this irritating beeper clipped to my purse. How do I act relaxed, knowing that at any minute the little monster will start beeping. If that happens, it means that I must be at the data center in 30 minutes flat. Yes, it's nice to feel wanted and important, but not *this* week!

"Finding that IMS application bug took most of the week, and I'm bushed! Lying on the sand, sipping a beer, reading a trashy novel — that's just what I need now. After all, it's Saturday.

"Elizabeth, why don't you and I go for a dip? The waves are low, and we can rinse some of this sand off of us. I know the waves are sometimes scary, but I'll hold your hand and ..."

B-E-E-E-E-E-P

Appendix

Miscellaneous Reference Section

GLOSSARY OF TERMS

This list represents many of the acronyms that a mainframe MVS programmer encounters. Some are used in this book, some are not.

ABEND (ABnormal END)
ALC (Assembler Language Code)
AMS (Access Method Services)
ANSI (American National Standards Institute)
APAR (Authorized Program Analysis Reports)
BAL (see ALC)
BLL (Base Locator for Linkage Section)
BTS (Batch Terminal Simulator — for use with IMS)
CICS (Customer Information Control System)
CMS (Conversational Monitor System)
COBOL (COmmon Business Oriented Language)
COBTEST (COBOL testing facility)
DASD (Direct Access Storage Device)
DBCS (Double Byte Character Set)
DB2 (Database 2)

DFP	(Data Facility Product)
DFSORT	(Data Facility Sort)
DL/I	(Data Language/I — see IMS/VS)
EBCDIC	(Extended Binary Coded Decimal Interchange Code)
HDAM	(Hierarchical Direct Access Method for IMS)
HIDAM	(Hierarchical Indexed Direct Access Method for IMS)
IMS	(See IMS/VS)
IMS/VS	(Information Management System/Virtual Storage)
ISPF	(Interactive Structured Programming Facility)
JCL	(Job Control Language)
JES	(Job Entry Subsystem)
MVS/ESA	(Multiple Virtual Storage/Enterprise Systems Architecture)
MVS/SP	(Multiple Virtual Storage/System Product)
MVS/XA	(Multiple Virtual Storage/Extended Architecture)
NJE	(Network Job Entry)
PDS	(Partitioned Data Set)
PL/1	(Programming Language/I)
PTF	(Program Temporary Fix)
QMF	(Query Management Facility)
QSAM	(Queued Sequential Access Method)
RACF	(Resource Access Control Facility)
REXX	(Restructured Extended Executor)
RMF	(Resource Measurement Facility)
SAA	(Systems Application Architecture)
SQL	(Structured Query Language)
TSO	(Time Sharing Option)
TGT	(Task Global Table — a COBOL term)

VSAM (Virtual Storage Access Method)
VTAM (Virtual Telecommunications Access Method)

SKILL MATRIX FOR TYPICAL CAREER POSITIONS

This chart (Figure A.1) represents common software skills in an MVS shop. Some of the software products may not be installed at your company. Also, this is not a hard and fast chart that should be followed explicitly. The focus of this chart is not on developing a training program but on emphasizing the wide

Legend: X = Good working knowledge needed
B = Basic competency needed
C = Conceptual skills needed

MVS SKILLS	Programmer IMS	DB2	CICS	MIS Manager	End-User	MIS Analyst
JCL	X	X	X	B	C	B
Link Editor	X	X	X	C	C	B
Utilities	X	X	X	C		B
TSO	X	X	X	B	B	B
ISPF	X	X	X	B	B	B
CLISTs	X	X	X	B		B
REXX	X	X	X	C		B
COBOL	X	X	X	B		B
COBTEST	X	X	X	C		X
QMF		X		B	B	X
DB2		X		B		B
IMS	X			B	C	B
CICS			X	B	C	B
VSAM			X	B		B
BTS	X			C		X
Dump reading	X	X	X	C		
PC Interfaces		X	X	C	C	B

Figure A.1. Example of MVS skills matrix.

variety of skills that a person must possess to use MVS effectively. To ignore any of these skills is to unnecessarily increase your company's costs of using MVS.

If you noticed that I suggest MIS managers need to know basic JCL and ISPF (plus some other skills), you're right. Managers who cannot monitor their programmer's work environment are unable to fulfill an important part of their responsibility: ensuring that their staff has a productive set of tools.

PUBLICATIONS AVAILABLE

Chapter 6 reviewed the option to learn MVS with a planned reading program. While many classroom courses are available, your own reading is still an excellent way to learn. Since both QED and IBM have an extensive offering of MVS reference books, I prepared this listing to simplify your task of identifying those books that are of interest to you. This is a personally developed list and does not necessarily reflect the opinion of QED or of IBM. What all these books have in common is that each of them will help you learn and use MVS. Happy reading!

From QED

These books (as well as a complete catalog) may be ordered directly from QED. These books are hands-on, aimed at the reader who wants to master MVS. Each is a thorough reference in its subject. More specialized books are also available.

MANAGEMENT CONCERNS AND PLANNING:

IBM's Repository Manager/MVS by Dr. Henry C. Lefkovits

Migrating to DB2 by Lockwood Lyon

DB2: The Complete Guide to Implementation and Use by Jeff D. Vowell

MASTERING THE FUNDAMENTALS:

MVS/JCL: Mastering Job Control Language by Gabriel F. Gargiulo

APPENDIX: MISCELLANEOUS REFERENCE SECTION

MVS/TSO: Mastering Native Mode and ISPF by Gabriel F. Gargiulo

ENHANCING MVS ENVIRONMENTAL PROGRAMMING SKILLS:

MVS/TSO: Mastering CLISTs by Barry K. Nirmal

REXX in the TSO Environment by Gabriel F. Gargiulo

MASTERING MVS PROGRAMMING ENVIRONMENTS:

MVS COBOL II Power Programmer's Desk Reference by David Shelby Kirk

Embedded SQL for DB2: Application Design and Programming by Jonathan S. Sayles

PL/1 Programmer's Guide to Embedded SQL for DB2 by Jonathan S. Sayles

USING DB2 AND SQL FACILITIES:

SQL for DB2 and SQL/DS Application Developers by Jonathan S. Sayles

QMF: How to Use Query Management Facility with DB2 and SQL/DS by Gabriel F. Gargiulo and Jonathan S. Sayles

TUNING MVS APPLICATIONS FOR OPTIMUM PERFORMANCE:

DB2: Maximizing Performance of Online Production Systems by W.H. Inmon

VSAM: The Complete Guide to Optimization & Design by Eugene S. Hudders

IMS Design and Implementation Techniques, 2nd Edition by T. Jack McElreath

DB2 Design Review Guidelines by W.H. Inmon

From IBM

IBM produces over 300 manuals for each of their MVS versions. Obviously, you will never read them all, nor should you. IBM provides this service because MVS is complex, and many technical professionals must have access to explicit information. As a manager or application programmer or systems user, you will never need information of that depth. What I have done here is list the material that is probably adequate to propel you beyond the stage of wondering what MVS is all about to do your job effectively. I deliberately avoided describing technical manuals, as you will discover your need for them as you progress through your MVS-related career. Reminder: Before ordering any IBM manuals, check with your technical staff for the appropriate version. Those listed here may not be the correct ones for your shop.

Also, you should know that IBM does an admirable job of keeping material currrent and usually provides a manual of general information for each new software product. That means that you should look for such new publications each time your company makes major upgrades to software, such as moving from CICS/OS/VS to CICS/MVS, or from MVS/XA to MVS/ESA.

Some books are mutually exclusive, each having been written for a specific software environment. In those situations, the books are enclosed in brackets. The needed text depends on which software your company uses. For example, the following indicates that the two books are mutually exclusive:

> SC33-0241, *CICS/OS/VS Application Programmer's Reference*
>
> SC33-0512, *CICS/MVS Application Programmer's Reference*

Whenever you use IBM manuals, you should check that the release level of the book corresponds with the level of software you are using. For example, if your shop is using COBOL II, Release 3.0, and your COBOL II manuals reflect support for Release 3.1 or 3.2, there will be features in the manual that won't function. Likewise, if your library's JCL manual specifies MVS/SP and you are using MVS/XA, there will be features available that are unfamiliar. When in doubt, check with your technical staff.

Note: If you are an MIS manager, one of your top priorities should be to ensure that your staff has an up-to-date reference library and that it is readily available. The time that programmers waste searching for manuals far exceeds the cost of the manuals. If a programmer spends just 30 minutes searching for a reference text, the cost of the book will have been exceeded by the cost of lost productivity. If the programmer needs the reference again, the loss continues to increase. (If your company uses non-IBM software, the problem typically gets worse. For whatever reason, when companies acquire non-IBM software, there is a tendency to purchase only a handful of reference manuals for the staff. This doesn't help the programmers learn how to use the software.)

FOR MANAGERS AND NONTECHNICAL PERSONNEL

(or persons new to the MVS environment but who are otherwise computer-literate):

GC28-1823, *An Introduction to MVS*

GC26-4341, *SAA Overview*

GC23-0049, *MVS/XA JES3 Introduction*

GC28-1500, *MVS/XA General Information Manual*

GC28-1600, *MVS/ESA General Information Manual*

GC26-4275, *IMS/ESA General Information Manual*

GC33-0155, *CICS/ESA General Information Manual*

GC26-4073, *DATABASE 2 General Information Manual*

GG24-1581, *IBM DB2 Relational Concepts*

GG24-3404, *MVS/ESA Data in Memory Concepts*

GR20-4787, *MVS/ESA 31-Bit Addressing*

FOR PROGRAMMERS AND OTHER TECHNICAL PERSONNEL:

For programming with Assembler H:

GA22-7000, *IBM System/370 Principles of Operation*

GC26-4037, *Assembler H Language Reference*

SC26-4036, *Assembler H Application Programming Guide*

GC26-4014, *MVS/XA Data Administration Macro Instruction Reference*

GC28-1154, *MVS/XA Supervisor Services and Macro Instructions*

For programming with COBOL II:

GC26-4047, *VS COBOL II Language Reference*

SC26-4045, *VS COBOL II Application Programming Guide*

SC26-4049, *VS COBOL II Debugging*

SX26-3721, *VS COBOL II Reference Summary*

SC26-4301, *Report Writer Programmer Guide*

FOR SAA:

SC26-4354, *SAA Common Programming Interface, COBOL Reference*

GC26-4675, *SAA Common Programming Interface, Summary*

For CICS:

SC33-0241, *CICS/OS/VS Application Programmer's Reference*

SC33-0512, *CICS/MVS Application Programmer's Reference*

APPENDIX: MISCELLANEOUS REFERENCE SECTION

SC33-0226, *CICS/OS/VS Rel 1.7 Messages and Codes*

SC33-0514, *CICS/MVS Messages and Codes*

SC26-4177, *IMS/VS Version 2 Application Programming for CICS Users*

SC26-4080, *IBM Database 2 Application Programming Guide for CICS Users*

For IMS:

SH20-9026, *IMS/VS Version 1 Application Programming*

SH26-4178, *IMS/VS Version 2 Application Programming*

SH20-9030, *IMS/VS Version 1 Messages & Codes*

SC26-4174, *IMS/VS Version 2 Messages & Codes*

SH20-5523, *IMS/VS Batch Terminal Simulator Program Reference*

For DB2:

SC26-4380, *IBM Database 2 SQL Reference*

SC26-4293, *IBM Database 2 Application Programming Guide*

SC26-4292, *IBM Database 2 Advanced Application Programming Guide*

For MVS System Services:

GC28-1300, *MVS/SP JCL Reference*

GC28-1352, *MVS/XA JCL Reference*

GC28-1829, *MVS/ESA JCL Reference*

GC38-1008, *MVS/SP System Codes*

GC28-1157, *MVS/XA System Codes*

GC28-1815, *MVS/ESA System Codes*

GC28-1374 and GC28-1375, *MVS/SP System Messages*

GC28-1376 and GC28-1377, *MVS/XA System Messages*

GC28-1812 and GC28-1813, *MVS/ESA System Messages*

GC26-4061, *MVS/SP Linkage Editor & Loader User's Guide*

GC26-4011, *MVS/XA Linkage Editor & Loader User's Guide (Ver. 1)*

GC26-4143, *MVS/XA Linkage Editor & Loader User's Guide (Ver. 2)*

SC33-4035, *DFSORT Application Programming: Guide*

GC26-4051, *MVS/370 Access Method Services Reference*

GC26-4019, *MVS/XA Access Method Services Reference (Ver. 1)*

GC26-4135, *MVS/XA Access Method Services Reference (Ver. 2)*

GC26-4074, *MVS/SP VSAM Administration: Macro Instruction Reference*

GC26-4016, *MVS/XA VSAM Administration: Macro Instruction Reference (Ver. 1)*

GC26-4152, *MVS/XA VSAM Administration: Macro Instruction Reference (Ver. 2)*

GC26-4065, *MVS/370 Data Administration: Utilities*

GC26-4018, *MVS/XA Data Administration: Utilities (Ver. 1)*

GC26-4150, *MVS/XA Data Administration: Utilities (Ver. 2)*

Index

3380 disk drive, 19

Access method, 15, 16
Accounting, 30
Address space, 64, 93
APPC, 96
AS/400, 96
ASP, 70
Assembler H, 92
Assembler language, 40, 97
Attached System Processor, 69
Autocoder, 39

Batch, 1
Bootstrap process, 37
BTS, 77
Burroughs B-5500, 66

Catalog, 21
CBT, 104
CICS, xvii, 25, 82
CLISTs, 29
COBOL II, 92
Command lists, 29
Computing capacity, 14
Controllers, 18
CPU, 2
CRT, 75

DASD, 19, 20
Data Facility Product (DFP), 99
Data/Language I (DL/I), 76
Database, 2
DATABASE 2, 84
Dataset, 2, 7
DB2, xvii, 16, 84
DD statement, 61
Device-independence, 23
DFP, 99
DFSORT, 99
Distributed processing, 96
Data management, 15
Dump, 51

EXEC, 62
  CICS, 84

File, 2
First generation, 38
Flowchart, 8

Generation, 38
Gigabytes, 92
Glossary, 113

HASP, 69
Hierarchical data structures, 85

123

Houston Automatic Spooling
  Priority system (HASP), 69
I/O channels, 18, 52
IEBCOPY, 59
IEBGENER, 59
IEBTPCH, 59
IMS data structures, 77
IMS, xvii, 16, 76
IMS/DC, 25, 79
Information Management
  System, 76
Initial Program Load (IPL), 57
Input Output Control System
  (IOCS), 41
Interrupts, 48
IPL, 57
ISAM, 71
ISPF, xvii, 29, 75

JCL, 5
JES, 4
JES2, 69
JES3, 70
Job Control Language (JCL), 5
Job Entry Subsystem (JES), 4, 69
Job, 3, 36
  management, 3
JOBLIB, 62

Kilobytes, 65

Languages, 39
Library, 42
Linkage Editor, 59
LINKLIB, 61
Linklist, 62
Load module, 59
Logical database, 81
LU 2.0, 95
LU 6.2, 95

Macro-level coding, 40
Megabyte, 65
MFT, 63
Multiple Virtual Storage
  (MVS), 1, 47, 64, 92

Multiprocessing, 93
Multiprogramming, xvii, 14, 44
MVS, xvii, 1, 47, 64, 92
  /DFP, 99
  /ESA, 92
  /SP, 92
  /XA, 92
MVT, 63

Normal forms, 86
Normalization, 86

Online, 1
Operating System (OS), 47
OS, 47
  /2, 96
  /360, 56
  /400, 96

Pages, 67
Partitioned dataset, 61
PDS, 61
PGMLIB, 61
PROCLIB, 62

QED, 8, 81, 95
QMF, 87
Query Management
  Facility (QMF), 87

RACF, 29
RCA Spectra, 68
Readers, 68
Redundant data, 80
Region, 65
Register, 54
  -displacement concept, 53
Relational data structures, 85
Repository, 95
Response time, 13
Resource Access Control Facility
  (RACF), 29
Restructured Extended Executor
  (REXX), 29
REXX, 29

Second generation, 38
Security, 29

INDEX

Skill matrix, 115
SNA, 95
SQL, 84
Step, 4
Structured Query
  Language (SQL), 84
Supervisor Call (SVC), 52
SVC, 52, 64
Sysplex, 93
System
  flowcharts, 8
  task, 26
  /360, 44, 47, 55
  /370, 55
Systems Complex, 93
  Network Architecture
    (SNA), 95
  programmers, 7

Task management, 10
Telecommunications, 24, 95
Third generation, 38
Thrashing, 67
Time Sharing Option
  (TSO), 28, 75

Time-sharing, 28
Transaction, 24
  management, 27
TSO, 28, 75

Utilities, 58

VDT, 75
Virtual
  memory, 66
  Storage Access
    Method, (VSAM) 16
  Telecommunications Access
    Method (VTAM), 24
VOLSER, 21
Volume serial number, 21
Volume table of contents
  (VTOC), 21
VS1, 64
VS2, 64
VSAM, 16 82
VTOC, 21

Writers, 68

RESPONSE FORM

Book: *The World of MVS*

I want to hear from you. You may have questions, you may find errors, or you may have comments that will help me develop the next edition of the book. The purpose of this book is to help you, the MVS user, programmer, or manager. Thank you.

                                      David Shelby Kirk

Dear Dave,

_____

_____

_____

_____

_____

_____

_____

_____

_____

_____

_____

_____

_____

If a reply is desired, please fill in your address:

Name: _____

Address: _____

City, State: _____ Zip: _____

Mail to: David S. Kirk, c/o QED Information Sciences, PO Box 82-181, Wellesley, MA 02181